HARNESSING THE POTENTIAL OF BIG DATA IN POST-PANDEMIC SOUTHEAST ASIA

MAY 2022

ASIAN DEVELOPMENT BANK

© 2022 Asian Development Bank
6 ADB Avenue, Mandaluyong City, 1550 Metro Manila, Philippines
Tel +63 2 8632 4444; Fax +63 2 8636 2444
www.adb.org

Some rights reserved. Published in 2022.

ISBN 978-92-9269-511-8 (print); 978-92-9269-512-5 (electronic); 978-92-9269-513-2 (ebook)
Publication Stock No. TCS220186
DOI: http://dx.doi.org/10.22617/TCS220186

The views expressed in this publication are those of the authors and do not necessarily reflect the views and policies of the Asian Development Bank (ADB) or its Board of Governors or the governments they represent.

ADB does not guarantee the accuracy of the data included in this publication and accepts no responsibility for any consequence of their use. The mention of specific companies or products of manufacturers does not imply that they are endorsed or recommended by ADB in preference to others of a similar nature that are not mentioned.

By making any designation of or reference to a particular territory or geographic area, or by using the term "country" in this document, ADB does not intend to make any judgments as to the legal or other status of any territory or area.

Please contact pubsmarketing@adb.org if you have questions or comments with respect to content, or if you wish to obtain copyright permission for your intended use that does not fall within these terms, or for permission to use the ADB logo.

Corrigenda to ADB publications may be found at http://www.adb.org/publications/corrigenda.

Notes:
In this publication, "$" refers to United States dollars.
ADB recognizes "South Korea" as the Republic of Korea.

On the cover: The wide range of big data applications holds immense opportunities for optimizing public service delivery in health care, social welfare and protection, and education. For instance, in the Philippines, the development of a central identification platform can be useful for targeting beneficiaries of social protection programs.

Cover design by Cleone Baradas.

Contents

Tables, Figures, and Boxes

Foreword

This publication is the last of four reports from a regional study completed in 2021 and funded by the technical assistance of the Asian Development Bank (ADB) on Policy Advice for COVID-19 Economic Recovery in Southeast Asia. The project supports the recovery efforts of Southeast Asian countries to return to their economic performance before the coronavirus disease (COVID-19) pandemic. It also assists countries in preparing for national, regional, or global transformations that may take place post-COVID-19. The focus countries are Cambodia, Indonesia, Myanmar, the Philippines, and Thailand, which tapped ADB's COVID-19 Pandemic Recovery Option facility.[*] The study produced four reports on the following thematic areas:

1. **Supporting post-COVID-19 economic recovery in Southeast Asia.** After analyzing different sectors, their potential for growth, and the strengths of economies in Southeast Asia, ADB identified five key sectors: tourism, agro-processing, and garments are well-established sectors needing transformation or improvement; while electronics and digital trade are evolving sectors with a high potential for growth. This allows the development of more targeted policies given the constraints to governments' financial and administrative resources.
2. **Strengthening domestic resource mobilization in Southeast Asia.** COVID-19 exacerbated the struggles of some governments to generate tax revenue to meet public expenditure needs. ADB proposes policy actions to expand the tax base, increase tax compliance, and strengthen tax administration to create a healthy fiscal space.
3. **Implementing a green recovery in Southeast Asia.** Green recovery from the pandemic is crucial to ensure an economically and environmentally resilient future for Southeast Asia. Well-designed policy measures can simultaneously achieve socioeconomic and environmental goals.
4. **Harnessing the potential of big data in post-pandemic Southeast Asia.** Digitalization gained more prominence amid COVID-19 and highlighted the value of big data for the effective and efficient delivery of key public services such as health care, social welfare and protection, and education. A range of policy enablers for big data adoption in policy making—from strategic governance to building a data driven culture—were examined.

This publication provides policy makers with a baseline to understand the scope of policy options available in their pursuit of economic recovery. There is still much uncertainty on timing, particularly as the trajectory of the pandemic (i.e., new COVID-19 mutations) remains unclear and countries await the development and distribution of more vaccines. While COVID-19's impact on Southeast Asia has been significant, the report provides hope. The medium-term growth opportunities are strong. Taking advantage of those opportunities, however, will require a significant rethink of current approaches. This series of publications will hopefully inspire governments to think beyond the containment stage and lay the groundwork for opportunities that will ensure a sustainable recovery underpinned by more resilient economies and societies.

The research benefited from the insights and perspectives of government officials, the private sector, the academe, and other key stakeholders and experts working in the region who convened in thematic workshops, roundtable consultations, and focus group discussions. We are grateful for their support and collaboration.

---

[*]   ADB's stance on Myanmar since 1 February 2021 is outlined in its public statements of 2 February 2021 and 10 March 2021.

The ADB resident mission offices of the focus countries have effectively coordinated all country consultations to inform the study. We look forward to ADB's continued engagement with these countries, in line with its current approaches, to carry out the policy recommendations to support the region's recovery efforts. These recommendations align with the operational directions on fostering regional cooperation and integration under ADB's Strategy 2030. Strengthening regional cooperation is crucial for dealing with future crises more effectively.

Ramesh Subramaniam
Director General
Southeast Asia Department
Asian Development Bank

Acknowledgments

The research was supported by the regional technical assistance on Policy Advice for COVID-19 Economic Recovery in Southeast Asia (TA 9964). The team from the Regional Cooperation and Operations Coordination Division (SERC), Southeast Asia Department (SERD) of the Asian Development Bank (ADB) led by Thiam Hee Ng, former principal economist, SERC, with support from Dulce Zara and Georginia Nepomuceno, managed the study and coordinated the preparation of this publication under the supervision of Alfredo Perdiguero, director, SERC. Jason Rush provided technical support. Maria Theresa Bugayong and Hannah Estipona extended administrative assistance.

The study is a collaboration between ADB and AlphaBeta (SG) PTE LTD led by Fraser Thompson. Konstantin Matthies and Mai Lan Hoang from AlphaBeta prepared the report. Several ADB staff provided invaluable comments, including Arndt Husar, Amir Jilani, Thomas Abell, Seok Yong Yoon, Arturo Martinez, Marc Lepage, David Freedman, Jay Roop, Chitchanok Annonjarn, Teresa Mendoza, and Mohd Sani Moh Ismail.

The team gratefully acknowledges the views and suggestions of government officials, the private sector, the academe, researchers, development partners, and other stakeholders. They generously extended their support and cooperation during the thematic workshops, roundtable consultations, focus group discussions, and related events during the Southeast Asia Development Symposium 2021 that was conducted as part of the stakeholder engagement for this undertaking. Special thanks to the ADB resident missions in Cambodia, Indonesia, Myanmar, the Philippines, and Thailand for coordinating the participation of in-country stakeholders in the workshops and consultation meetings. Very thoughtful insights were also provided by Ramonette Serafica, Jose Ramon Albert, Francis Quimba, Andrew Staples, Sriganesh Lokanathan, Deborah Elms, and Jude Michael.

Effective 1 February 2021, ADB placed a temporary hold on sovereign project disbursements and new contracts in Myanmar. The bank continues to monitor the situation in the country. All of the background assessments in this study were undertaken before 1 February 2021.

The Knowledge Support Division of ADB's Department of Communications facilitated the publishing of this study.

Abbreviations

ADB	Asian Development Bank
AI	artificial intelligence
API	application programming interface
ASEAN	Association of Southeast Asian Nations
BA	Bundesagentur für Arbeit
CamDX	Cambodia Data Exchange
COVID-19	coronavirus disease
DEPA	Digital Economy Promotion Agency
DGA	Digital Government Development Agency
DICT	Department of Information and Communications Technology
GDP	gross domestic product
GPS	global positioning system
ICT	information and communications technology
IT	information technology
MGI	McKinsey Global Institute
NEXT	nurturing expert talent
OBR	online business registration
SDG	Sustainable Development Goal
UN	United Nations
WHO	World Health Organization

Executive Summary

Every day and everywhere, vast quantities of data from a wide range of sources are being generated at an exponential pace. The increasing use and rapid advancement of digital technology have created a data explosion that can be harnessed to transform critical public sector functions. Although the potential of big data has long been recognized, the coronavirus disease (COVID-19) pandemic has brought it to the fore. Public institutions have turned to big data because of its analytical power to turn voluminous datasets into actionable insights that can help them respond swiftly to crises, improve their services, and enhance resilience to future shocks. In particular, in response to the COVID-19 pandemic and the subsequent recovery, big data holds immense promise for optimizing public health, education services, and social protection, thereby expediting countries' post-pandemic recovery.

Health Care

In the health care sector, there is a large amount of data from health records that can be leveraged for big data analyses. This database can be combined with data from other sources such as social media, smartphone applications, and remote monitoring systems to support policies related to the prevention, detection, and treatment of diseases. Data-driven technologies, particularly big data applications, could help improve the delivery of health care services and reduce costs. Across Southeast Asia, the benefits of rolling out data-driven public health interventions and remote patient monitoring alone are estimated to be worth $24.9 billion annually by 2030.

For the focus countries, there are three main areas of opportunity where big data can be particularly useful in the health care sector. First, it can be used to improve the monitoring of infectious disease outbreaks. For example, it can be employed for preventative health surveillance by monitoring the health conditions of populations to detect possible epidemics before they occur. Second, it could enhance the prevention and detection of noncommunicable diseases. For example, United Nations (UN) Global Pulse (an initiative by the UN to bring big data and artificial intelligence to development programs) and the World Health Organization showed the potential of using big data to monitor risk factors associated with noncommunicable diseases (e.g., tobacco and alcohol use, diet, and physical activity). Finally, it can help improve treatment capacity through remote patient monitoring. For instance, big data-reliant devices can help alert physicians when there are potential issues such as heart failure.

Social Welfare and Protection

In the social welfare and protection sector, the COVID-19 pandemic has highlighted the need to improve the delivery of social welfare and protection programs. In the Philippines, ₱207 billion ($4.2 billion) was allocated as of December 2020 to the Department of Social Welfare and Development for cash assistance to low-income families.[1] However, there are a number of existing challenges that have affected the targeting and delivery of social assistance programs (e.g., lack of reach to the informal sector and inadequate granularity

---

[1] Government of the Republic of the Philippines. Investor Relations Office. https://iro.ph/articledetails.php?articleid=3617&catid=11.

of poverty data). For example, many informal sector workers in Cambodia who have lost their jobs due to COVID-19 cannot benefit from the government's cash support due to their unregistered status.[2]

Big data has three applications that can address the challenges in the development and delivery of social welfare and protection programs. First, it could help in identifying beneficiaries. A study conducted by the UN Global Pulse and World Food Program on the Tabasco flood in Mexico found that real-time information derived from mobile phone usage patterns can help authorities and humanitarian agencies pinpoint areas of acute need with a high level of speed and precision.[3] Second, it could improve program delivery and detect fraud. For instance, rule-based algorithms can flag suspicious correlations such as a person receiving unemployment benefits while filing for a work-related accident. Third, it could help in assessing program effectiveness. For example, using anonymized financial account data from banks or digital wallet providers allows the analysis of household behavior shifts after receiving cash transfers and how this money was spent.

Education

In the education sector, there is a potential to make use of social media platforms as well as online job portals which provide a large amount of data on jobs and skills trends. While student records are not yet fully digitized in most countries, the increasing adoption of online learning solutions has presented valuable opportunities for obtaining insightful data for education policies. For example, many educational institutes in Southeast Asia shifted to online learning platforms during the COVID-19 pandemic. Such initiatives to expand the adoption of digital technologies help build a foundation for applying data-driven analytics in the focus countries. The benefits brought about by data-driven technologies, such as personalized learning and online job matching, are estimated at an annual $77.1 billion across Southeast Asia by 2030.

There are three main areas where big data can be particularly useful in the education sector. First, big data can help in identifying skill gaps. For example, data from online job portals can be analyzed to understand employment and skill trends and develop training courses that respond to industry needs. Second, big data could help increase graduation rates and prevent dropouts. By leveraging big data analytics, schools can look into the vast number of student records to identify early warning signs and provide targeted support to those in need. Finally, big data could provide a personalized learning experience to cater to the unique needs of students. For instance, by collecting data on how students interact with the virtual learning environment, the online sources they use for research, their participation in chats and forums, the areas that they struggle with, as well as the way they present information, schools can have a better understanding of their abilities and learning styles.

Policy Enablers

However, to unlock the potential of big data in public service delivery, seven policy enablers would be required. These are (i) strategic governance, (ii) availability and quality of data, (iii) risk mechanisms, (iv) human capital for big data, (v) access to relevant technologies, (vi) data-driven culture, and (vii) information and communications technology (ICT) infrastructure.

Digitizing public sector data and accessing big data is growing and advancement in technologies could facilitate wider application. However, governments need to lay the strategic and technical groundwork to maximize the opportunities of big data and mitigate its risks, including protection for data privacy, fraud, and cyber-security.

---

[2]   UN. 2020. *UN Cambodia Framework for the Immediate Socio-Economic Response to COVID-19.* https://unsdg.un.org/sites/default/files/2020-09/KHM_Socioeconomic_Response-Plan_2020.pdf.

[3]   UN Global Pulse. *Guest Post: Mobile Phone Data Analysis for Disaster Management.* https://www.unglobalpulse.org/project/online-signals-for-risk-factors-of-non-communicable-diseases-ncds/.

Big data can support over $100 billion worth of opportunities across the five focus countries

COVID-19 has presented a number of challenges for governments in Southeast Asia

Cost of health spending due to COVID-19 in Southeast Asia is estimated at **~0.4–0.5%** of GDP

Across Asia Pacific, the negative impact of COVID-19 is expected to push an additional **78 million** households below the poverty line, reversing over **50%** of the progress on poverty reduction over the last 5 years

Youth unemployment rate in Southeast Asia could increase by **2x** from pre-COVID-19 levels, adding **4 million** unemployed

Big data can improve the delivery of government services during COVID-19 and speed up the post-COVID-19 recovery

Application of remote monitoring systems could bring **$9.4 billion** in annual cost savings to the health care system of Southeast Asian countries by 2030 through reduced hospital visits, length of patients' stays and medical procedures

Use of analytics to direct highly targeted health interventions for at-risk populations could lead to an increase of **$15.5 billion** in GDP across Southeast Asian countries by 2030

Use of digital technologies to provide personalized and remote learning as well as online job matching could contribute **$77.1 billion** annually to GDP of Southeast Asian countries by 2030

Five key opportunities for using big data in health care, social welfare and protection, and education

1.
Analyzing COVID-19 activity

2.
Supporting vaccine rollout

3.
Monitoring noncommunicable diseases

4.
Targeting vulnerable populations

5.
Identifying skills gap

Seven areas of policy reform could help capture these opportunities

Strategic governance	Data availability	Risk mechanisms	Human capital	Relevant technology	Data-driven culture	ICT infrastructure

COVID-19 = coronavirus disease 2019, GDP = gross domestic product, ICT = information and communications technology.
Source: Authors.

SECTION I

Introduction

Digital technologies are transforming the global economy. In Southeast Asia, the size of the internet economy for the first time crossed the $100 billion mark in 2019.[1]

By 2025, the value of Southeast Asia's internet economy could triple to $300 billion. The broader impact on the rest of the economy could, however, be far larger than this. It is estimated that Southeast Asia's digital economy[2] has the potential to increase annual regional gross domestic product by $1 trillion through 2025 as compared to 2015.[3] Governments are actively trying to drive this digital transformation, foster the growth of their digital economy, and leverage a range of technologies to improve public service delivery. Big data and other technologies that build on it such as artificial intelligence (AI) can play a transformative role in the public sector. In particular, in the response to the coronavirus disease (COVID-19) pandemic and the subsequent recovery, big data can generate unique insights and help public institutions stay on top of the wide range of challenges they are facing.

This section focuses on big data applications and opportunities in three public service sectors—health care, social protection and assistance, and education. These three sectors were selected as the focus of this report for two reasons: (i) their importance in the economic recovery from COVID-19 and building resilience to future pandemics and (ii) their relevance for policy makers (informed by consultations with policy makers in the focus countries). A set of enabling factors that are crucial for deriving the maximum value from big data for governments are then discussed and finally, a set of recommendations, including pilots and policy reforms, are outlined to help countries capture the big data opportunity.

---

[1]   Bain & Company. 2020. *e-Conomy SEA 2020.* https://www.bain.com/insights/e-conomy-sea-2020/.

[2]   This includes 10 Southeast Asian countries: Brunei Darussalam, Cambodia, Indonesia, Lao People's Democratic Republic, Malaysia, Myanmar, the Philippines, Singapore, Thailand, and Viet Nam.

[3]   A. T. Kearney and Axiata. 2016. *The ASEAN Digital Revolution.* https://www.kearney.com/documents/20152/5364057/ The+ASEAN+digital+revolution.pdf/625da4b5-8d05-6798-004a-e49a59e8d817?t=1581504740845.

Big Data and Big Data Analytics

▶ **Big data presents large opportunities for public service improvements.**

Simply put, big data refers to datasets whose size is beyond the ability of typical database software tools to capture, store, manage, and analyze (Box 1 provides further details on the definition of big data).

Box 1: What are Big Data and Big Data Analytics?

"Big data" refers to datasets whose size is beyond the ability of typical database software tools to capture, store, manage, and analyze.[a] This incorporates an evolving definition of how big a dataset needs to be in order to be considered big data as the size of datasets that qualify as big data will increase as technology advances over time. Depending on what kinds of software tools are commonly available and what sizes of datasets are used in a particular industry, big data can range from a few dozen terabytes to multiple petabytes (thousands of terabytes). Some practitioners consider a set of data "big" if its size is larger than the size of their computer's processing power.

"Big data analytics" refers to the process of collecting, organizing, and analyzing big data to discover trends and patterns in large amounts of raw data to help make data-informed decisions. The collection and storage of big data have been facilitated by cloud computing which allows larger storage capacity, faster computing power, and flexible scaling of resources without the need for on-premises hardware. Meanwhile, the process of analyzing big data requires new data analysis methods such as data mining (i.e., looking through large datasets to identify patterns and relationships by identifying anomalies and creating data clusters), predictive analytics (i.e., using an organization's historical data to make predictions about the future and identify upcoming risks and opportunities), and deep learning (i.e., a subset of artificial intelligence which involves using multiple layers of neural network algorithms to find complex patterns in various datasets). This is enabled by a number of tools and technologies, some of which are open-source and can be leveraged for cost-effective rollouts of big data applications (e.g., the Apache Software Foundation, a nonprofit organization promoting collaborative open-source software development, provides a range of open-source tools to support the execution of data-oriented applications such as Ignite, Spark, and Storm).[b]

[a] McKinsey Global Institute. 2011. Big Data: The Next Frontier for Innovation, Competition, and Productivity. https://www.mckinsey.com/~/media/McKinsey/Business%20Functions/McKinsey%20Digital/Our%20Insights/Big%20data%20The%20next%20frontier%20for%20innovation/MGI_big_data_full_report.pdf.
[b] Apache Software Foundation (ASF). https://www.apache.org/foundation/.

Three are four drivers influencing the potential value of big data by sector:
- **Volume of data.** The larger the amount of data in the sector, the more it indicates the potential to benefit from utilizing big data analytics. This depends not only on the volume of potential data, but how much is currently digitized.
- **Variety of data.** The more different forms of data available in the sector (e.g., social media, video content, and structured data), the more potential value there could be in combining them to generate unique insights.
- **Veracity of data.** The higher the quality or accuracy of the data, the better the potential insights.
- **Value of applications.** The degree to which there are specific applications in that sector that can deliver value.

Our research has shown that the opportunity for capturing value from big data in three public service sectors—health care, social welfare and protection, and education—is significant (Table 1; see Table A1 of Appendix 1 for detailed methodology). In the health care sector, for example, there is a large amount of data from health records that can be leveraged for big data analyses. This database can be combined with data from other sources such as social media, smartphone applications, and remote monitoring systems to support policies related to prevention, detection, and treatment of diseases. In the education sector, there is a potential to make use of social media platforms as well as online job portals which provide a large amount of data on jobs and skills trends. While student records are not yet fully digitized in most countries, the increasing adoption of online learning solutions has presented valuable opportunities for obtaining insightful data for education policies. For example, most schools in Indonesia shifted to online learning platforms during the COVID-19 pandemic. The transition was supported by the Ministry of Education and Culture which partnered with EdTech companies to provide free access to online learning platforms and with telecommunications operators to provide free internet quotas for teachers and students.[4] Meanwhile, in the Philippines, the government issued a memorandum to close the gap in resources and facilities in "last mile schools," including improving internet connection and installing computerized program packages, even before the COVID-19 pandemic.[5] Such initiatives to address the digital divide and expand the adoption of digital technologies help build a foundation for applying data-driven analytics in the focus countries. Regarding data on social assistance

Table 1: Capturing the Benefits from Big Data in Health Care, Social Welfare and Protection, and Education

Assessment on criteria: ■ High ■ Medium ■ Low

Sectors	Volume of Data	Variety of Data	Veracity of Data	Value of Applications
Health care	Large potential amount of data, but much is still not digitized	Large potential variety of data from electronic medical records, population studies, remote monitoring systems, social media, smartphone applications, etc.	Veracity of data varies– strong for medical records and population studies, but weaker in other areas (e.g., social media)	Large number of case studies of benefits across prevention, detection, and treatment of both infectious diseases and noncommunicable diseases
Social welfare and protection	Potentially large (e.g., through increasing use of mobile phones). Beneficiary information varies in terms of digitalization, but growing through the use of digital payments	Large potential variety of data, ranging from poverty studies to government payment information and mobile phone data	Veracity of data varies– records of past beneficiary payments are generally strong, but reliance on satellite data or mobile phone data can be rough proxies	Large potential benefits in the development, implementation, and monitoring of social assistance programs
Education	Large potential amount of data, particularly with online job boards listing real-time job and skills demand information	Large potential variety of data, including academic records, online job boards, and EdTech solutions	Veracity of data varies– strong for academic records, but there are some challenges with other forms of data (e.g., quality of data from online job boards may vary)	Large potential benefits in terms of understanding jobs and skills trends to enable effective education and training policies as well as providing personalized learning

Source: AlphaBeta analysis.

---

4   D. Gupta and N. Khairina. 2020. COVID-19 and Learning Inequities in Indonesia: Four Ways to Bridge the Gap. *World Bank Blogs*. 21 August. https://blogs.worldbank.org/eastasiapacific/covid-19-and-learning-inequities-indonesia-four-ways-bridge-gap.

5   Government of the Philippines, Department of Education. https://www.deped.gov.ph/2019/05/22/may-22-2019-dm-059-s-2019-prioritizing-the-development-of-the-last-mile-schools-in-2020-2021-reaching-out-and-closing-the-gap/.

programs and beneficiaries, while the current level of digiization varies by country, there are opportunities to derive insights from alternative data sources such as satellite data and mobile phone data.

A. Digital Economy Trends

▶ **Big data applications in health care can improve the monitoring of infectious diseases, enhance the prevention and detection of noncommunicable diseases, and improve treatment capacity.**

Prior to COVID-19, total government expenditure on health care in Southeast Asian countries was estimated at between 0.8% and 3.4% of the gross domestic product (GDP) of these countries.[6] Health care spending in the region has significantly increased due to the COVID-19 pandemic. For example, Indonesia reallocated Rp 27 trillion ($1.8 billion) to fund the health care system in March 2020 to manage the impact of the pandemic, and announced a plan to reallocate additional budget to provide free vaccines to Indonesians.[7] Data-driven technologies, particularly big data applications, could help improve the delivery of health care services and reduce costs. Across Southeast Asia, the benefits of rolling out data-driven public health interventions and remote patient monitoring alone are estimated to be worth $24.9 billion annually by 2030 (Figure 1; see Table A2.1 of Appendix 2 for detailed methodology).

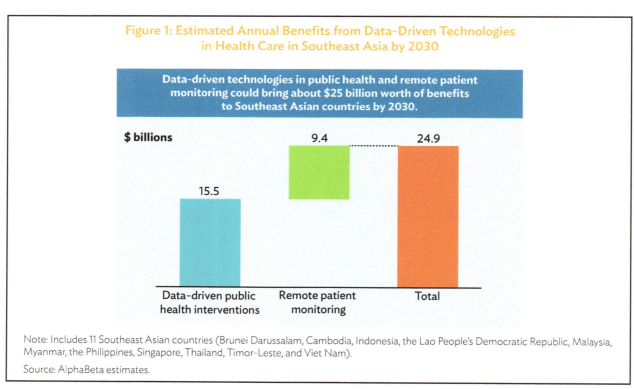

Figure 1: Estimated Annual Benefits from Data-Driven Technologies in Health Care in Southeast Asia by 2030

Data-driven technologies in public health and remote patient monitoring could bring about $25 billion worth of benefits to Southeast Asian countries by 2030.

$ billions

15.5	9.4	24.9
Data-driven public health interventions	Remote patient monitoring	Total

Note: Includes 11 Southeast Asian countries (Brunei Darussalam, Cambodia, Indonesia, the Lao People's Democratic Republic, Malaysia, Myanmar, the Philippines, Singapore, Thailand, Timor-Leste, and Viet Nam).

Source: AlphaBeta estimates.

---

[6]   ADB. 2020. *Key Indicators for Asia and the Pacific 2020*. Manila. https://www.adb.org/sites/default/files/publication/632971//ki2020.pdf.
[7]   A. Akhlas. 2020. Indonesia to Reallocate $1.8b Budget for Health Care, Cash Transfers: Sri Mulyani. *The Jakarta Post*. 18 March. https://www.thejakartapost.com/news/2020/03/18/indonesia-to-reallocate-1-8-budget-for-health-care-cash-transfers-sri-mulyani.html; L. Yulisman. 2020. Indonesia to Offer Free Covid-19 Vaccines to All, President Joko to Get it First. *The Straits Times*. 16 December. https://www.straitstimes.com/asia/se-asia/indonesia-to-offer-free-vaccines-to-all-president-joko-to-get-it-first.

B. Leveraging Big Data for Public Service Delivery

1. Health Care

For the focus countries, there are three main areas of opportunity where big data can be particularly useful in the health care sector—(i) improving the monitoring of infectious disease outbreaks; (ii) enhancing the prevention and detection of noncommunicable diseases; and (iii) improving treatment capacity through remote patient monitoring.

- **Improving the monitoring of infectious diseases.** Ensuring effective health service delivery has become even more critical in light of the COVID-19 pandemic. For example, more than 1 million people across the five focus countries have been infected with the virus as of December 2020.[8] As a result, health systems of these countries are faced with a number of difficulties that affect their ability to manage infectious disease outbreaks. For instance, the Ministry of Health of Cambodia and the World Health Organization (WHO) have identified deficiencies in the country's prevention and detection capacities, including human resource constraints, a lack of capacity for case detection and contact tracing, and challenges in health emergency coordination at subnational levels.[9] There are several ways in which big data can play a role in the monitoring of infectious diseases. Big data can be employed for preventative health surveillance by monitoring health conditions of populations to detect possible epidemics before they occur. For instance, data from smartphone-connected thermometers can allow for real-time tracking of influenza activity. A study analyzing data from over eight million temperature readings generated by almost 450,000 smartphone-connected thermometers used by households[10] in the United States showed that the data were highly correlated with information obtained from traditional disease surveillance systems and could potentially predict influenza activity up to 2 to 3 weeks in advance.[11] Furthermore, search engines and social media are also valuable data sources that can help detect the emergence of possible epidemics. In a study that collected data of Google searches and Twitter messages related to influenza in Greece and compared them against official statistics, it was found that Google and Twitter data produced precise estimates of the influenza development and had the potential to predict influenza before it is observed in the population.[12] Big data has also been essential for contact tracing during the COVID-19 pandemic. Data from mobile phones, transport systems, or social media can be used to identify location and track travel patterns of diagnosed or suspected cases to support disease tracking and provide early warning for populations at risk. A number of countries have leveraged location data (e.g., global positioning system [GPS] data) and Bluetooth data from mobile phones for contact tracing during the pandemic. For instance, Singapore's TraceTogether app collects proximity data based on exchanges of Bluetooth signals to identify people who have prolonged proximity with infected cases.[13] Box 2 provides another example of using big data for contact tracing and surveillance in the Republic of Korea. In addition, countries can also stay one step ahead by leveraging big data to support the delivery and implementation of vaccines. Big data can be used to ensure that vaccines are stored within a precise range of temperatures, preserving their quality from the manufacturer to the point of use. For example, Merck collaborated with Microsoft to analyze and monitor a range of variables that could affect the cold chain,

---

[8]   WHO. WHO Coronavirus Disease (COVID-19) Dashboard. https://covid19.who.int/ (accessed 10 December 2020).

[9]   ADB. 2020. *Report and Recommendation of the President to the Board of Directors: COVID-19 Active Response and Expenditure Support Program.* Manila.

[10] The study used data from commercially available Kinsa Smart Thermometers which record and store temperature measurements, using the Kinsa smartphone application. When recording temperatures, users can assign readings to profiles by age and sex, allowing readings from multiple users within a household to be distinguished. Readings are geocoded using Global Positioning System location (for enabled devices) or by Internet Protocol address.

[11] A. Miller et al. 2018. A Smartphone-Driven Thermometer Application for Real-Time Population and Individual-Level Influenza Surveillance. *Clinical Infectious Diseases.* 67 (3). pp. 388–397.

[12] L. Samaras et al. 2020. Comparing Social Media and Google to Detect and Predict Severe Epidemics. *Scientific Reports.* 10 (1). pp. 1–11.

[13] TraceTogether. https://www.tracetogether.gov.sg/index.html.

including origin, destination, delivery route, external weather, and logistics providers.[14] In another partnership between Google.org—the charitable arm of Google—and Gavi, a wireless temperature monitoring system called ColdTrace was built to provide real-time data on refrigerators used to store vaccines.[15] The system collects data from sensors placed inside vaccine refrigerators and will notify key personnel when vaccines are in danger.[16] Regarding the implementation of vaccination programs, big data can be used to identify priority populations such as particularly vulnerable groups (e.g., elderly people with preconditions) and "super spreaders" (i.e., individuals with high levels of close contact with many others such as those working in the service industry). Box 3 shows an example of an application used to identify vulnerable populations in the early days of the COVID-19 pandemic, which can be deployed for vaccination programs. When it comes to mass vaccination campaigns, data from social media platforms can be used to understand public perceptions and concerns around vaccines, and develop strategies to address them.

Box 2: Leveraging Big Data for Disease Surveillance during COVID-19 in the Republic of Korea

Ten minutes is all it takes for the Republic of Korea authorities to track the travel history of a coronavirus disease (COVID-19) patient using big data, compared to about 1 day if a manual epidemiological survey were used. This is enabled by the COVID-19 smart management system (SMS), a system that leverages big data provided by 28 organizations, including the police, credit card companies, and telecom service providers.

Jointly developed by the Korea Centers for Disease Control and Prevention, the Ministry of Land, and the Ministry of Science and ICT, the system was rolled out in March 2020, a month after the number of cases spiked. The system analyzes a person's credit card transactions and mobile phone location records to instantly map out a virus transmission route and identify potential infection hot spots. Big data was used in combination with direct interviews of the infected people. This allowed Korea Centers for Disease Control and Prevention to identify and isolate potential cases early, and openly share risk alerts to help other citizens stay safe. By relying on aggressive contact tracing and widespread testing, the Republic of Korea was able to contain the outbreak without resorting to drastic measures such as blanket lockdowns.

Source: C. Chang. 2020. How South Korea Used Tech to Track Down Coronavirus and Curb Spread. *The Straits Times*. 1 May. https://www.straitstimes.com/asia/east-asia/how-south-korea-used-tech-to-track-down-virus-and-curb-spread.

- **Enhancing the prevention and detection of noncommunicable diseases.** There are longer term pressures on each country's health care system such as the rising burden of noncommunicable diseases. In Thailand, for example, the prevalence of noncommunicable diseases (e.g., cardiovascular diseases, cancers, diabetes, and chronic respiratory diseases), driven by the country's high level of alcohol and tobacco use, has become a pressing public health issue.[17] Similarly, the contribution of noncommunicable diseases to Indonesia's total health loss[18] has increased from 39.7% in 1990 to 72.3% in 2019, exposing the population to greater

---

[14] N. Bragazzi et al. 2018. Vaccines Meet Big Data: State-of-the-Art and Future Prospects. From the Classical 3Is ("Isolate–Inactivate–Inject") Vaccinology 1.0 to Vaccinology 3.0, Vaccinomics, and Beyond: A Historical Overview. *Frontiers in Public Health*. 6. p. 62.

[15] S. Berkley. 2017. How Innovation Is Improving Vaccine Delivery. *LinkedIn*. 21 November. https://www.linkedin.com/pulse/how-innovation-improving-vaccine-delivery-seth-berkley/.

[16] Nexleaf Analytics. https://nexleaf.org/vaccines/#what-is-coldtrace.

[17] UNDP. 2020. *Multi-Sectoral Approaches to NCDs in Thailand.* https://www.undp.org/content/undp/en/home/librarypage/hiv-aids/multi-sectoral-approaches-to-ncds-in-thailand.html.

[18] Total health loss is a measure of how much healthy life is lost due to early death, illness, or disability as a result of certain health conditions and their consequences.

risks when hit by pandemics such as COVID-19.[19] Big data can play an important role in the prevention and detection of health risks related to noncommunicable diseases. One project collected data from hospitals and population studies of five European countries and used it to detect the risk of developing diabetes in a given population (Box 4). In another example, United Nations (UN) Global Pulse (an initiative by the United Nations to bring big data and artificial intelligence to development programs) and the WHO showed the potential of using big data to monitor risk factors associated with noncommunicable diseases (e.g., tobacco and alcohol use, diet, and physical activity). The study found that indices for risk factors could be built and tracked over time on social media such as Twitter. Internet search traffic using keywords such as "stop smoking" could also be analyzed to provide faster and cheaper information on noncommunicable diseases.[20]

Box 3: Analyzing Big Data to Identify Priority Populations for Vaccination Programs

Big data can be used to identify priority populations for vaccination programs such as people with pre-existing chronic diseases and those working in the service industry. For example, Blue Shield of California, an insurer in the United States, used big data analysis to identify clients who were most vulnerable to coronavirus disease (COVID-19).[a] The company leveraged a machine learning platform to analyze different factors such as individuals' health history combined with social, environmental conditions, and the most up-to-date medical literature on COVID-19. This helped identify a number risk factors that could have been overlooked such as location (e.g., individuals who did not live within a close-enough vicinity to a grocery store were at an increased risk of ending up in the hospital, on a ventilator, or even dying from COVID-19) and underlying conditions (e.g., individuals who had experienced severe mental health issues were at greater risk). Based on these findings, Blue Shield was able to provide targeted health counseling and support services to its members, including free meal delivery, medication delivery, telemedicine, and in-home clinical visits.

[a] G. Velasquez. 2020. The COVID-19 Vaccine Rollout is Dangerously Flawed. Science and Data Could Fix It. *Fortune.* 19 December. https://fortune.com/2020/12/18/covid-vaccine-rollout-ai-data-science-machine-learning/.

Box 4: Using Big Data to Support the Prevention and Detection of Diabetes in Europe

MOSAIC is a European Union-funded project aimed at providing an innovative approach for the diagnosis and management of diabetes by leveraging big data.[a] Multiple databases from hospitals, local health agencies, and population studies across five European countries were integrated and used as the basis for building predictive models to support the prevention and detection of diabetes. The project created a tool that allows health administrators and hospitals in a given geographic area to analyze a selected population and see shares of the population that are at risk of developing type 2 diabetes within the next 2 to 10 years. At the individual level, the current risk of each patient can be assessed, allowing health managers to detect patients that are at high risk of developing the disease and focus diagnostic tests on those cases. Moreover, by enabling better detection and diagnosis of diabetes in the early stages, the system allows authorities to start prevention activities such as promoting healthy lifestyles early.

[a] MOSAIC Project. 2016. MOSAIC Overview Presentation. http://www.mosaicproject.eu/images/MOSAIC_PRESENTATION_2016.pdf.

---

[19] A. Syakriah and D. Septiari. 2020. Rising Noncommunicable Diseases Loom Over Nation's COVID-19 Fight. *The Jakarta Post.* 17 October. https://www.thejakartapost.com/news/2020/10/17/rising-noncommunicable-diseases-loom-over-nations-covid-19-fight.html.

[20] UN Global Pulse. Online Signals for Risk Factors of Non-Communicable Diseases (NCDs). https://www.unglobalpulse.org/project/online-signals-for-risk-factors-of-non-communicable-diseases-ncds/.

- **Improving treatment capacity through remote patient monitoring.** When it comes to the treatment of diseases, the lack of facilities and lack of human resources are critical challenges across many countries in Southeast Asia, which have been exacerbated during the pandemic. For example, with only eight hospital beds per 10,000 persons, Cambodia is faced with a shortage of facilities, particularly at the national and provincial levels.[21] Meanwhile, in the Philippines, the limited number of health care workers, at only 17 health care workers (four doctors, nine nurses, and four midwives) per 10,000 persons, is a major constraint leading to low treatment capacity.[22] Systems that leverage big data to improve treatment capacity through remote patient monitoring can include devices that monitor heart conditions and blood-sugar levels and then feed data in near real-time to electronic medical record databases. They can also alert physicians when there are potential issues such as heart failure. The use of data from remote monitoring systems can improve productivity, reduce patient in-hospital bed days, and cut emergency department visits. A study conducted by Singapore General Hospital in 2019, which piloted vital signs trackers (including a blood pressure cuff and biosensor) among a group of patients, showed significant productivity improvements. As compared to in-person checks, approximately 9 minutes were saved by remotely monitoring a patient hourly for 6 hours, and up to 22 minutes were saved when the hourly monitoring stretched across 12 hours.[23] Remote patient monitoring has been shown to have significant economic impact through reduced hospital visits, length of patients' stays, and medical procedures. The McKinsey Global Institute (MGI) estimates savings of 10%–20% to health care systems from the resultant reduced hospital visits, length of patients' stays, and number of procedures of applying remote patient monitoring systems. Applying this impact to Southeast Asia's context, one could expect cost reductions of $9.4 billion annually by 2030.

As assessment of the extent of big data usage in health care across the five focus countries reveals several important initiatives. For example, Thailand's Ministry of Public Health highlighted the use of big data as one of the major reforms in its eHealth Strategy (2017–2026).[24] The ministry is also encouraging hospitals under its supervision to tap the power of big data in tackling challenges in the prevention and treatment of diseases. Meanwhile, in Indonesia, social media data were analyzed to provide real-time insights on public perceptions on immunization in a study conducted by the Ministry of Development Planning (Bappenas), Ministry of Health, United Nations Children's Fund, WHO, and Pulse Lab Jakarta.[25] In particular, analysis of relevant conversations on Twitter shed light on public concerns around immunization such as religious issues and side effects of vaccines. The data obtained from public tweets helped identify a network of Twitter influencers (accounts with a large number of engaged followers) that could be leveraged by public health practitioners for rapid response to public concerns and misinformation related to vaccines and immunization.

2. Social Welfare and Protection

▶ **Social protection and assistance schemes can leverage big data during design, delivery, and review of programs.**

The COVID-19 pandemic has highlighted the need to improve the delivery of social welfare and protection programs. In the Philippines, ₱35 billion ($730 million) was allocated to aid displaced workers through cash-for-work and other forms of assistance while ₱241 billion ($5 billion) was allocated to the Department of

---

[21]   World Health Organization data. https://www.who.int/data/gho/data/indicators/indicator-details/GHO/hospital-beds-(per-10-000-population).

[22]   ADB. 2020. *Report and Recommendation of the President to the Board of Directors: Health System Enhancement to Address and Limit COVID-19.* Manila.

[23]   SingHealth. *Why Remote Monitoring Will Shape Tomorrow's Medicine.* https://www.singhealth.com.sg/news/tomorrows-medicine/why-remote-monitoring-will-shape-tomorrows-medicine.

[24]   Ministry of Public Health. 2017. *eHealth Strategy (2017–2026).* Nonthaburi: Information and Communication Technology Center.

[25]   UN Global Pulse. 2014. *Understanding Public Perceptions of Immunisation Using Social Media.* https://www.unglobalpulse.org/wp-content/uploads/2014/08/understanding-public-perceptions-of-immunisation-using-social-media.pdf.

Social Welfare and Development for cash assistance in areas under lockdown.[26] Cambodia also launched the Cash Transfer Program for Poor and Vulnerable Households during COVID-19 to provide a monthly allowance to poor households affected by the pandemic, with total spending estimated at KR100–KR120 billion ($25–$30 million) per month.[27] In addition, $100 million was allocated to a cash-for-work program to absorb the labor force who have lost employment from the factories or enterprises and returned home from the foreign countries while a monthly allowance of $40 will be given to each worker in the garment and tourism industries until March 2021.[28] However, there are a number of existing challenges that have affected the effectiveness of social assistance programs (e.g., lack of reach to the informal sector and partial coverage of poverty data). For example, many informal sector workers in Cambodia who have lost their jobs due to COVID-19 cannot benefit from the government's cash support due to their unregistered status.[29]

Social protection and assistance programs in Asia and the Pacific will come under further strain in the years to come. While developing countries in the region have seen tremendous progress on extreme poverty reduction over the last decade (from 1.1 billion or 33.5% of the population in 2002 to 263 million or 6.9% in 2015), COVID-19 is estimated to have reversed over 50% of the progress on poverty reduction in the last 5 years, seeing 78 million additional people above pre-COVID-19 estimates slip back into extreme poverty in 2020 alone (Figure 2).[30]

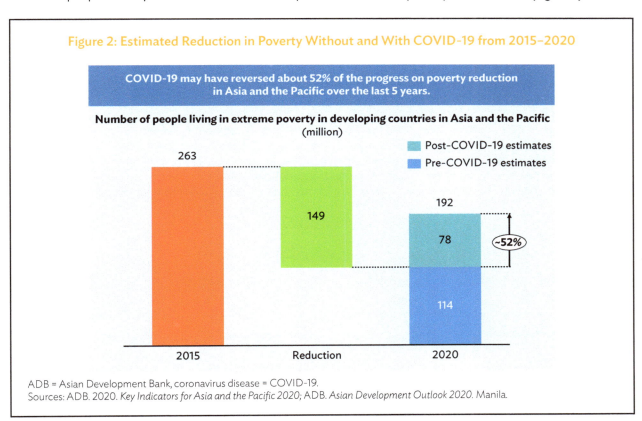

Figure 2: Estimated Reduction in Poverty Without and With COVID-19 from 2015–2020

COVID-19 may have reversed about 52% of the progress on poverty reduction in Asia and the Pacific over the last 5 years.

Number of people living in extreme poverty in developing countries in Asia and the Pacific (million)

ADB = Asian Development Bank, coronavirus disease = COVID-19.
Sources: ADB. 2020. *Key Indicators for Asia and the Pacific 2020*; ADB. *Asian Development Outlook 2020*. Manila.

[26] Government of the Philippines, Department of Budget and Management. https://www.dbm.gov.ph/index.php/programs-projects/status-of-covid-19-releases.

[27] Office of the Council of Ministers. *Selected Comments Samdech Techo Hun Sen, Official Launch of Cash Transfer Program for Poor and Vulnerable Households during Covid-19*. https://pressocm.gov.kh/en/archives/66499.

[28] ADB COVID-19 Policy Database. Cambodia. https://covid19policy.adb.org/index.php/policy-measures/CAM (accessed 20 January 2021).

[29] UN. 2020. *UN Cambodia Framework for the Immediate Socio-Economic Response to COVID-19*. https://unsdg.un.org/sites/default/files/2020-09/KHM_Socioeconomic_Response-Plan_2020.pdf.

[30] ADB. 2020. *Key Indicators for Asia and the Pacific 2020*. https://www.adb.org/sites/default/files/publication/632971/ki2020.pdf; and ADB. 2020. *Asian Development Outlook 2020*. https://www.adb.org/sites/default/files/publication/635666/ado2020-update.pdf.

Big data has several applications that can address challenges in the development and delivery of social welfare and protection programs, including better targeting of beneficiaries and improving the design of these programs through more tailored interventions. These include:

- **Identifying beneficiaries.** In addition to the increased need for social protection and assistance, there exist major challenges that may hinder the impact of social welfare and protection response in the focus countries. For example, while Thailand provides a relatively high level of social protection and is making use of electronic payments to improve service delivery, the country is faced with challenges in identifying target populations, particularly for the Child Support Grant which offers cash to households with children less than 6 years old and the Social Welfare Card which provides transport and gas subsidies as well as subsidies on food and other necessities to low-income individuals at designated stores. The fragmented and inconsistent management of social protection data, coupled with limited coordination among government agencies, have resulted in information silos and affected the accuracy of targeting.[31] In the Philippines, the lack of granularity of poverty data obtained from household surveys is a key constraint in identifying populations living under poverty, particularly in remote areas.[32] Identifying which segments of the population should be targeted with social assistance programs can be difficult in the absence of frequently updated databases on the socioeconomic conditions of different groups. Alternative data sources such as cell phone data or satellite imagery can complement official statistics by providing more granular and updated insights into vulnerable populations. Such innovative datasets have supported important applications in poverty reduction as well as disaster risk management. For example, in a World Bank's project in Guatemala, cell phone call records were analyzed to assess users' socioeconomic behavior, including consumption, mobility, and social patterns, to produce poverty estimates that were more cost-effective and updated than traditional survey data.[33] Innovative data sources could also play a vital role in disaster response and recovery. For instance, a study conducted by the UN Global Pulse and World Food Program on the Tabasco flood in Mexico found that real-time information derived from mobile phone usage patterns can help authorities and humanitarian agencies pinpoint areas of acute need with a high level of speed and precision.[34] By analyzing millions of aggregated and de-identified mobile phone datasets, the research team was able to map the flow of people moving across a region, identify the most damaged areas, and gain insights into affected populations. Table 2 provides further examples of how data from mobile phone operators can be used to improve the targeting of vulnerable populations.

Table 2: Examples of Big Data from Mobile Phone Operators for Targeting Vulnerable Populations

Network/Usage Data	Relevance for Targeting
Handset (manufacturer, brand, and how frequently it is changed or upgraded)	Price of handset as proxy for income
Mobility between cell sites (including internationally)	Travel patterns and movements between regions
Top-up amount, denomination, and frequency	Monthly expenditure and usage as proxy for socioeconomic status
Use of services and applications (e.g., voice, SMS, data, 2G, 3G, and 4G)	Basic education or literacy profile and consumption propensity
Branchless banking remittances (inward and outward)	Estimation of receipts or payments to augment income estimation

Source: AlphaBeta analysis.

---

[31]   UNICEF. 2020. *Social Impact Assessment of COVID-19 in Thailand.* https://www.unicef.org/thailand/media/5071/file/Social%20Impact%20Assessment%20of%20COVID-19%20in%20Thailand.pdf.

[32]   ADB. 2020. *Mapping Poverty through Data Integration and Artificial Intelligence: A Special Supplement of the Key Indicators for Asia and the Pacific.* Manila.

[33]   World Bank Group. 2017. *Estimating Poverty Using Cell Phone Data.* https://openknowledge.worldbank.org/bitstream/handle/10986/26136/WPS7969.pdf?sequence=1&isAllowed=y.

[34]   UN Global Pulse. *Guest Post: Mobile Phone Data Analysis for Disaster Management.* https://www.unglobalpulse.org/project/online-signals-for-risk-factors-of-non-communicable-diseases-ncds/.

- Another potential application of big data involves analyzing existing social welfare and protection programs to identify gaps and improve the design of these programs. In particular, governments can analyze records of past beneficiaries, results of the interventions and use these insights to develop tailored programs. Box 5 provides a case study on the usage of big data in managing unemployment benefits and job placement services.

Box 5: Improving the Management of Unemployment Benefits and Job Placement Services Using Big Data

The Bundesagentur für Arbeit (BA) or the Federal Employment Agency is the provider of labor market services in Germany with a network of 156 employment agencies and approximately 600 branches nationwide.[a] The agency is responsible for providing job placement and career counseling, promoting vocational and further training, and distributing unemployment benefits.

To improve its services, BA analyzed a large amount of historical data of its customers, including the histories of unemployed workers, the interventions that were implemented, as well as the outcomes (e.g., how long it took people to find a job). Based on this analysis, the agency was able to evaluate the characteristics of its unemployed and partially employed customers and develop a segmented approach that offered more effective placement and counseling services to targeted customer segments. After analyzing the outcome data of its placement programs, BA identified programs that were ineffective and removed or refined them using new approaches.

This allowed the agency to optimize its programs and reduce total spending by €10 billion ($12 billion).[b] The amount of time that unemployed workers took to find employment was also reduced, leading to higher satisfaction ratings.

[a]   Bundesagentur für Arbeit. https://www.arbeitsagentur.de/.
[b]   McKinsey Global Institute. 2011. *Big Data: The Next Frontier for Innovation, Competition, and Productivity*. https://www.mckinsey.com/~/media/McKinsey/Business%20Functions/McKinsey%20Digital/Our%20Insights/Big%20data%20The%20next%20frontier%20for%20innovation/MGI_big_data_full_report.pdf.

- **Improving program delivery and detecting fraud.** Beyond providing an alternative source of data on at-risk populations, big data can also improve transparency and reduce risks of errors and fraud in identifying beneficiaries. This can be achieved by using algorithms to crawl through big data from a variety of sources to detect inconsistencies. For instance, rule-based algorithms can flag suspicious correlations such as a person receiving unemployment benefits while filing for a work-related accident. Other potential data sources such as bank statements or digital wallets can support the real-time refinement and tailoring of assistance provided to beneficiaries and optimize graduation or phasing out of cash transfers.

- **Assessing program effectiveness.** In the longer term, countries will also be required to strengthen their social welfare and protection efforts to extend other forms of support to the broader population in a post-COVID world (e.g., helping unemployed individuals or informal sector workers find new employment). Big data can be used to better evaluate the impact and success of social assistance programs. For example, using anonymized financial account data from banks or digital wallet providers allows the analysis of household behavior shifts after receiving cash transfers and how this money was spent. Similar approaches have been used in Australia to understand the impact of tax cuts on small business spending, using data from accounting software.[35]

There have been several initiatives across the five focus countries to leverage big data in the area of social welfare and protection; however, most are still at the exploratory or early phase. For example, a pilot study in the Philippines and Thailand that explored the use of satellite imagery in mapping poverty levels has shown the potential of using innovative data sources to complement traditional poverty statistics (Box 6). Meanwhile,

---

[35]   Xero & AlphaBeta. 2018. *Do Company Tax Cuts Boost Jobs, Wages and Investment?* https://www.alphabeta.com/wp-content/uploads/2018/05/Xero-SBI-AlphaBeta-Tax-Report_May-2018.pdf.

in Indonesia, the application of mobile data in mapping migration patterns was explored in a study conducted by Pulse Lab Jakarta and Bappenas in 2019. Using pseudonymous cellular data, the study provided a high level of granularity that allowed the Government of Indonesia to see the origins of individuals that migrated to large cities such as Jakarta, Medan, and Makassar. In addition to identifying migrant source communities and destination cities, the research also revealed essential insights on the volume and directional movements of rural to urban migration across Indonesia's vast archipelago.[36] The Government of Cambodia has also taken the first step in developing the infrastructure required to enable big data application in social welfare and protection. Led by the Ministry of Planning, the country implemented a digital identification system called "IDPoor" that serves as a single basis for targeting the poor population. This digital database has been used during the COVID-19 pandemic as a mechanism to identify more than 560,000 poor households for the "Cash Transfer Program for Poor and Vulnerable Households during COVID-19."[37] As a next step, "IDPoor" is planning to be integrated with databases from other government agencies such as the National Social Security Fund and the Ministry of Health to support the design and delivery of social welfare and protection programs in Cambodia.

Box 6: Mapping Poverty Levels in the Philippines and Thailand Using Satellite Imagery

Poverty statistics play a crucial role in identifying people who are at risk of socioeconomic exclusion and supporting the design of social protection programs. However, there are a number of challenges in the compilation of poverty statistics through household-based surveys. In particular, survey sample sizes are typically not large enough to provide reliable estimates at granular levels (e.g., municipalities and villages), and may, therefore, not be able to assist policy makers in efficiently targeting population segments that have the greatest need for poverty reduction programs. Furthermore, the relevance and timeliness of poverty statistics require that such surveys be conducted frequently, which can be costly for national statistics offices.

Big data can address these limitations by providing an alternative source of poverty estimates to complement traditional statistics. A study conducted by the Asian Development Bank (ADB) has shown the potential of using satellite imagery to generate richer insights on poverty levels. This approach was tested in two countries with different poverty profiles—the Philippines and Thailand, in collaboration with the countries' national statistics offices. Using machine-learning algorithms, the study predicted night-time light intensity, a proxy for human settlements and economic wealth, using daytime satellite images as input. It was found that even with publicly accessible satellite imagery, whose resolutions are not as fine as those in proprietary images, this method enabled more granular predictions of poverty levels than those currently being compiled by national statistics offices in both countries. The poverty map generated using satellite data has practical uses in mitigating the impact of coronavirus disease (COVID-19) such as identifying vulnerable households for food distribution.

Sources: Y. Sawada and E. Tan. 2020. Meeting Development Challenges with Trusted Data. *Asian Development Blog.* 20 October. https://blogs.adb.org/blog/meeting-development-challenges-trusted-data; and A. Martinez and A. Mehta. 2020. How Satellite Data Helped Get Food to the Hungry during COVID-19. *Development Asia.* 21 December. https://development.asia/explainer/how-satellite-data-helped-get-food-hungry-during-covid-19.

---

[36]   Pulse Lab Jakarta. 2019. *Annual Report.* https://www.unglobalpulse.org/wp-content/uploads/2020/05/PLJ-annual-report-2019.pdf.
[37]   UNICEF. *COVID-19 Cash Transfer Programme Helping Families with the Most Basic Needs.* https://www.unicef.org/cambodia/stories/covid-19-cash-transfer-programme-helping-families-most-basic-needs.

3. Education

▶ **The use of big data could transform outcomes in education and employment.**

COVID-19 has had a significant impact on employment in Southeast Asia. For example, youth across six Southeast Asian countries (Cambodia, Indonesia, the Lao People's Democratic Republic, the Philippines, Thailand, and Viet Nam) are expected to face a total of 4.3 million job losses in 2020 (Figure 3).

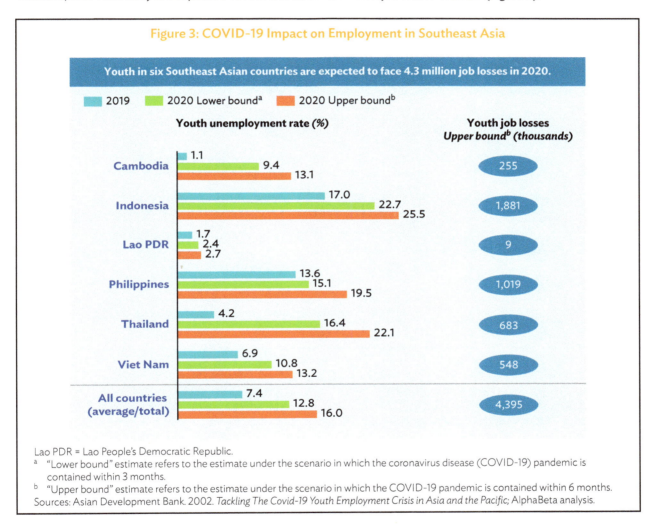

Figure 3: COVID-19 Impact on Employment in Southeast Asia

Lao PDR = Lao People's Democratic Republic.

a "Lower bound" estimate refers to the estimate under the scenario in which the coronavirus disease (COVID-19) pandemic is contained within 3 months.

b "Upper bound" estimate refers to the estimate under the scenario in which the COVID-19 pandemic is contained within 6 months.

Sources: Asian Development Bank. 2002. *Tackling The Covid-19 Youth Employment Crisis in Asia and the Pacific;* AlphaBeta analysis.

Much of the unemployment caused by COVID-19 could become long term as the pandemic has in many cases advanced underlying trends of retrenchment driven by automation and changes in the industry composition of economies. Certain types of workers across the five focus countries have been particularly affected by the COVID-19 pandemic—in particular, youth, informal workers, and migrant workers have experienced the largest unemployment impacts from the pandemic (Table 3). Youth, particularly graduates entering the labor force, face gloomy job market prospects as hiring activities decline. Young workers in employment before COVID-19 have been particularly affected as many are working in areas most impacted by the pandemic such as services. A global study by the International Labour Organization (ILO) found that one in six young people (17%) who

Table 3: Unemployment Impacts from COVID-19 by Type of Worker

Extent of negative impact on jobs:[a]   🟧 Large 🟨 Moderate 🟩 Limited 🟦 Limited applicability in country

Type of Worker	Cambodia	Thailand	Indonesia	Myanmar	Philippines
Youth	Large	Large	Large	Large	Large
Freelance workers	Limited applicability	Large	Large	Limited applicability	Large
Informal workers	Large	Large	Large	Large	Large
Domestic migrant workers	Large	Large	Large	Large	Large
Returning migrant workers from abroad	Large	Large	Large	Large	Large
Foreign workers	Moderate	Moderate	Limited	Moderate	Moderate
Women	Large	Large	Moderate	Large	Large
Aged workers	Limited applicability	Moderate	Moderate	Limited applicability	Limited applicability

COVID-19 = coronavirus disease.

[a]   "Large" refers to groups of workers that are assessed to have experienced significant unemployment impact due to COVID-19. "Moderate" refers to groups of workers that are assessed to have experienced some unemployment impact due to COVID-19. "Limited" refers to groups of workers that are assessed to be minimally affected by COVID-19.

Sources: Review of publicly available information on the impact of COVID-19 on employment; AlphaBeta analysis.

were employed before the outbreak, stopped working altogether, most notably younger workers aged 18–24.[38] Furthermore, freelance and informal workers whose income relies on ad hoc projects and daily work have been seeing a drastic decline in demand for their work. In addition to typically being accorded less priority in government COVID-19 policy, foreign workers face a range of newly imposed restrictions on work permits.

Education and skill development will be key tools for Southeast Asian countries to deal with this surge in unemployment and get affected populations back into the workforce. Beyond the need to reskill individuals impacted by the COVID-19 pandemic (where their roles may not return), there are also broader challenges facing the education sector in the long term such as ensuring the responsiveness of the education system to changing skill needs as well as increasing graduation rates. Data-driven applications could help address these challenges and improve the effectiveness of the education systems. The benefits brought about by such applications are estimated at an annual $77.1 billion across Southeast Asia by 2030 (Figure 4; see Table A2.2 of Appendix 2 for detailed methodology).

There are three main areas of big data applications that can help address challenges posed by the pandemic as well as improve the effectiveness and resilience of the education system in the long term. These include

---

[38]   ILO. 2020. *Youth and COVID-19: Impacts on Jobs, Education, Rights and Mental Well-Being.* https://www.ilo.org/wcmsp5/groups/public/---ed_emp/documents/publication/wcms_753057.pdf.

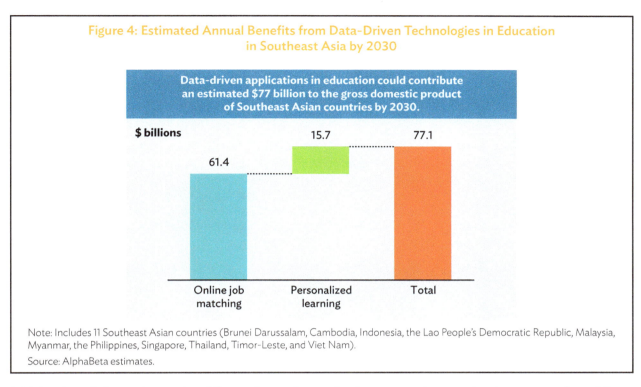

Figure 4: Estimated Annual Benefits from Data-Driven Technologies in Education in Southeast Asia by 2030

Data-driven applications in education could contribute an estimated $77 billion to the gross domestic product of Southeast Asian countries by 2030.

$ billions

Online job matching	Personalized learning	Total
61.4	15.7	77.1

Note: Includes 11 Southeast Asian countries (Brunei Darussalam, Cambodia, Indonesia, the Lao People's Democratic Republic, Malaysia, Myanmar, the Philippines, Singapore, Thailand, Timor-Leste, and Viet Nam).

Source: AlphaBeta estimates.

bridging the existing and emerging skills gap, increasing graduation rates and preventing dropouts, and providing a personalized learning experience for students.

- **Identifying skills gap.** Education is a key sector accounting for between 9% and 20% of total government spending in the five focus countries.[39] Yet, many Southeast Asian countries still experience significant mismatches between skill profiles generated by the education system and those demanded by the market. For example, Indonesia reported a skill gap due to the lack of industrial sectors' involvement in skills development and developing labor market information to capture emerging skills.[40] Cambodia, while having achieved notable progress in education, faces a worsening skills gap as the skills taught by technical and vocational education and training institutions do not appear to be adequately linked to those required by industry.[41] In the Philippines, the mismatch between jobs and skills has resulted in unemployment and underemployment among college-educated individuals.[42] This skills gap has widened due to COVID-19 as the pandemic has significantly accelerated digital transformation among businesses.[43] Digital skills such as using information technology (IT) tools, analyzing digital information, as well as collaborating the use of digital platforms are increasingly being a basic requirement across sectors. Big data can be used to address this skill mismatch through better skills gap identification, career advice, tailored learning, and better job matching as well as in developing a responsive education system in the long term. For example, data from online job portals can be analyzed to understand employment and skill trends and develop training courses that respond to industry needs. These job portals contain valuable information about job and skills demand by companies, which can offer complex insights into employers' needs according to sectors, professions,

---

[39] Our World in Data. *Share of Education in Government Expenditure, 1998 to 2018*. https://ourworldindata.org/grapher/share-of-education-in-government-expenditure?time=1998..latest&country=KHM~MMR~IDN~PHL~THA (accessed 10 December 2020).

[40] T. Muhamad and D. Sudono. 2020. Why Skills Development Is Even More Imperative for Indonesia. *The Jakarta Post*. 11 July. https://www.thejakartapost.com/academia/2020/07/11/why-skills-development-is-even-more-imperative-for-indonesia.html.

[41] P. Kanagaraj. 2019. Skills Gap Still Plagues Cambodia. *Capital Cambodia*. 5 April. https://capitalcambodia.com/skills-gap-still-plagues-cambodia/.

[42] C. Cudis. 2019. Labor, Employer Sectors Unite vs. Job Mismatch. *Philippine News Agency*. 11 July. https://www.pna.gov.ph/articles/1074716.

[43] P. Kuentak. 2020. New World of Work. *Bangkok Post*. 12 October. https://www.bangkokpost.com/business/2000635/new-world-of-work.

and types of skills.[44] Additionally, digital platforms such as LinkedIn and Facebook are increasingly becoming innovative recruitment channels, driven by growing opportunities for building relations and facilitating communication via social networks. With hundreds of millions of members, LinkedIn has the potential to offer a new, timely, and granular source of data about emerging industries, workers' changing skills composition, and how they are engaging with the labor market. The company has partnered with the World Bank Group in an initiative called "Digital Data for Development" to support innovative policy decisions in developing countries by providing insights on employment trends, skill needs, and skill adoption across industries, and talent migration.[45] Box 7 shows an example of how governments can make use of such data in developing education and training policies. Furthermore, some countries have leveraged emerging technology and analytics solutions to collect data on skills supply and demand, which can be used to develop education and training policies. An example of such initiative is Nurturing Expert Talent (NEXT) launched by TalentCorp, a national agency that is driving Malaysia's talent strategy. NEXT is a proprietary assessment system to help individuals identify their strengths, passion, and the career choices that are most suited to their skill sets.[46] The data gathered by the NEXT initiative could help TalentCorp shape future policies with evidence-based talent supply and demand data for key job roles.

Box 7: Using LinkedIn Data to Identify Skills Gap in South Africa

South Africa was faced with a critical task of managing double-digit unemployment rates and double-digit rates of individuals who were neither educated nor employed. The government, however, lacked the granular and actionable data on the types of talent and skills demanded by industry. To tackle this challenge, the World Bank partnered with LinkedIn to provide insights into the skills supply and demand in the country.

The analysis of LinkedIn data showed that South Africa had a strong global comparative advantage in traditional areas such as energy, mining, transport, and logistics and was slowly expanding as a regional leader in finance. However, the country lagged in sectors requiring digital skills (e.g., computer software and semiconductors). LinkedIn data also allowed for analysis of skill trends at subnational levels to identify unique growth capabilities of each region or city. For example, Cape Town's workforce was found to be competitive in areas related to business services, tourism, and creative work.

Based on the insights drawn from the analysis of LinkedIn data, policy makers were able to identify the most in-demand skills and develop strategies to produce a pipeline of talent in these areas. The low supply combined with strong demand for digital skills indicated significant upskilling and reskilling opportunities for the local workforce that would enable them to participate in the digital economy. The government also recognized the need to strengthen the education system from primary to tertiary levels to equip graduates with in-demand skills.

Sources: World Bank Group. 2018. *Data Insights: Jobs, Skills and Migration Trends Methodology & Validation Results.* https://development-data-hub-s3-public.s3.amazonaws.com/ddhfiles/144635/wbg-linkedin-methodology-report_1.pdf; and A. Fritzler, W. Flowerday, and J. Zhu. 2017. World Bank Partners with LinkedIn for Innovative Data and Insights on South Africa's Most In-Demand Skills. *World Bank Blogs.* 19 October. https://blogs.worldbank.org/psd/world-bank-partners-linkedin-innovative-data-and-insights-south-africas-most-demand-skills.

- **Increasing graduation rates and preventing dropouts.** Another issue pertinent to educators in the five focus countries is the need to provide timely support for disadvantaged and underperforming students to increase graduation rates and prevent dropouts. In Thailand, for example, results of the Programme for International Student Assessment indicated that socioeconomically advantaged students outperformed

---

[44]   European Commission. 2017. *Big Data for Monitoring Educational Systems.* https://euagenda.eu/upload/publications/untitled-102548-ea.pdf.
[45]   Digital Data For Development. https://linkedindata.worldbank.org/.
[46]   Epitome. *Improving Employment Outcomes for Graduates in Malaysia.* https://epitome.global/portfolio/improving-employment-outcomes-for-graduates-in-malaysia/.

disadvantaged students in all subjects, with many disadvantaged students displaying low ambition or self-confidence.[47] This is demonstrated by the fact that about one in six high-achieving disadvantaged students (versus one in 100 high-achieving advantaged students) do not expect to complete tertiary education.[48] Cambodia also saw a high dropout rate of 18% and low completion rate of 21% at the upper secondary level, with many students leaving schools with insufficient cognitive and workplace skills to meet expectations of employers (footnote 48). These problems are particularly dire in rural areas and among ethnic minority communities. In the long term, countries will need to improve the effectiveness of their education system and build capabilities to stay resilient to future shocks. Leveraging big data analytics, schools can look into the vast number of student records to identify early warning signs and provide targeted support to those in need. This application has been effectively adopted by Georgia State University in the United States to spot students who are at risk of dropping out even before they realize it and provide them with timely academic and financial support (Box 8).

Box 8: Georgia State University Leveraged Big Data to Prevent Dropouts and Increase Graduation Rates

Georgia State University saw a drop in graduation rates when it accepted more students with disadvantaged backgrounds, many of whom came from low-income families and were the first in their families to attend college.[a] While the university realized the need to provide support for students who were underperforming or facing financial issues, it lacked the resources to frequently monitor tens of thousands of students every semester (with only one adviser for every 1,000 students).

Big data presented an effective solution to their problem by pinpointing exactly which students required help and when. 140,000 student records containing 2.5 million grades from 10 years were analyzed to identify indicators for predicting when students might be in danger of dropping out or failing out.[b] This analysis enabled the university to identify 800 unique circumstances that increase the likelihood of dropping out such as poor academic results in first-year courses or late tuition fee payments. These insights were then used by advisers to develop targeted interventions to get students back on track. Students who might be in danger of dropping out would be contacted by an advisor within 48 hours for an in-person meeting. During the meeting, the adviser would probe to find out the student's particular challenges and help connect him or her with the appropriate resources (e.g., tutoring, emergency financial aid, or advice about other majors).

By utilizing big data in monitoring students' performance and understanding their specific situation, Georgia State University was able to increase graduation rates, especially among students from diverse racial, ethnic, and socioeconomic backgrounds.

[a] J. Barshay and S. Aslanian. 2019. Colleges are Using Big Data to Track Students in an Effort to Boost Graduation Rates, But It Comes At A Cost. *APM Reports.* 6 August. https://www.apmreports.org/episode/2019/08/06/college-data-tracking-students-graduation#:~:text=a%20Watchful%20Eye-,Colleges%20are%20using%20big%20data%20to%20track%20students%20in%20an,it%20comes%20at%20a%20cost&text=At%20Georgia%20State%20in%20Atlanta,its%20use%20of%20predictive%20analytics.
[b] Georgia State University. *Big Dreams, Big Data.* https://news.gsu.edu/2017/11/15/big-dreams-data/.

---

[47] OECD. 2018. *Programme for International Student Assessment (PISA)—Results from PISA 2018.* https://www.oecd.org/pisa/publications/PISA2018_CN_THA.pdf.

[48] ADB. 2018. *Report and Recommendation of the President to the Board of Directors: Second Upper Secondary Education Sector Development Program.* Manila. https://www.adb.org/projects/documents/cam-47136-006-rrp.

- **Providing personalized learning experience.** The COVID-19 pandemic had drastic implications for how teaching was conducted. In the Philippines alone, 25 million students had to be taught remotely at home.[49] But the switch to remote learning has posed major challenges. According to the World Economic Forum's Association of Southeast Asian Nations (ASEAN) Youth Survey 2020, 69% of youths aged between 16 and 35 in Southeast Asian countries found it difficult to work or study remotely, including 7% who said it was impossible. While 31% of survey respondents found working or studying from home easy, only 13% reported no constraints at all.[50] Big data can help make remote learning more effective. Educators can analyze data on students' learning styles, areas of interest, abilities, and progress to customize teaching methods and curriculums to individuals' needs. For example, by collecting data on how students interact with the virtual learning environment, the online sources they use for research, their participation in chats and forums, the areas that they struggle with, as well as the way they present information, schools can have a better understanding of their abilities and learning styles.[51] Personalized learning paths can be developed where students, depending on their abilities, interests, priorities, and progress can delve deeper into each subject with more relevant and effective learning methods. Arizona State University in the United States provides a good example of using big data to develop customized teaching methods. Standard lectures on the university's general level mathematics course were replaced with a "mathematics emporium," which involves students sitting at their computers and working through course content in their own time, with the help of tutors. Each student was placed at the appropriate starting point based on their abilities, and then continually assessed as they progressed through the course. As a result, the class' success rate increased from about 65% to 85%. The system can also integrate courseware from different classes to identify gaps and direct students to the specific parts that they need to revise (e.g., if an engineering student is struggling in a physics class because of a misunderstanding of calculus, they would be guided to revise relevant parts of the calculus syllabus).[52]

Across the five focus countries, the usage of big data in education is currently limited. One example of big data applications is observed in Thailand where data from job portals were leveraged to improve the responsiveness of the education system during the COVID-19 pandemic. In particular, its Ministry of Education funded an initiative to examine the labor market situation and build a database of skill needs using data from 12 online job portals. This enabled policy makers to identify skills gap and develop programs to re-train the workforce, particularly in digital skills required to operate during the pandemic.[53]

[49] AP. 2020. Asia Today: Remote Learning Begins In Virus-Hit Philippines. *AP News.* 5 October. https://apnews.com/article/virus-outbreak-pandemics-education-philippines-asia-9eed0f28ae8955940aa3aba73b2c644f.

[50] World Economic Forum. 2020. *COVID-19–The True Test of ASEAN Youth's Resilience and Adaptability Impact of Social Distancing on ASEAN Youth.* http://www3.weforum.org/docs/WEF_ASEAN_Youth_Survey_2020_Report.pdf.

[51] J. Ruiz-Palmero et al. 2020. Big Data in Education: Perception of Training Advisors on Its Use in the Educational System. *Social Sciences.* 9 (4). p. 53.

[52] H. Else. 2017. How Do Universities Use Big Data? *Times Higher Education.* 13 April. https://www.timeshighereducation.com/features/how-do-universities-use-big-data.

[53] W. Thearvanichpant. 2020. Big Data to Keep Thai Workers Afloat. *Thailand Development Research Institute.* 26 August. https://tdri.or.th/en/2020/08/big-data-to-keep-thai-workers-afloat/.

SECTION III

Key Enablers and Policy Actions to Maximize Potential of Big Data

▶ **Seven policy enablers are crucial to unlocking the full potential of big data in public service delivery.**

To capture the benefits of using big data, there is a need to create an enabling environment that enhances the availability and quality of data and encourages applications of big data analytics in government services. Seven policy enablers have been identified to support big data usage in government: (i) strategic governance, (ii) availability and quality of data, (iii) risk mechanisms, (iv) human capital for big data, (v) access to relevant technologies, (vi) data-driven culture, and (vii) ICT infrastructure.[54]

Based on these seven policy enablers and an assessment of a range of indicators, several improvement opportunities emerge for the five focus countries (Table 4; see Table A3 of Appendix 3 for detailed methodology).

The following section explains these seven policy enablers in detail and provides an assessment of the five focus countries with regard to each policy enabler.

- **Strategic governance.** From the outset, governments should create a clear plan, road map, or national strategy to foster the digital transformation of public services and promote the use of big data applications in public service delivery. For example, a lack of clear strategic focus related to digital technologies has been cited as one of the main themes preventing governments in Latin America to increase the adoption of cloud computing services.[55] The accountability should reside at senior levels of government. For example, as a signal of the importance of artificial intelligence, the United Arab Emirates appointed Omar Bin Sultan as the country's first Minister of State for Artificial Intelligence in 2017.[56] The current state of strategic governance for digital transformation varies across the five focus countries. Thailand has achieved notable progress in promoting e-government, with an established Digital Government Development Agency (DGA) which is in charge of providing services and support to all government agencies with regard to digital government transformation.[57] A number of initiatives have been implemented by DGA, including Government Cloud (cloud infrastructure for government agencies), e-Government Portal (a central information center to facilitate people in obtaining public services provided by different government agencies), and Government Information Network (a central government's information network that connects all government agencies to support various public services) (footnote 57). In addition, the Digital Economy Promotion Agency (DEPA) has been set up to promote digital technology adoption, and is already working with different government agencies in the country to help them understand big data and

54 McKinsey Global Institute. 2011. *Big Data: The Next Frontier for Innovation, Competition, and Productivity.* https://www.mckinsey.com/~/media/McKinsey/Business%20Functions/McKinsey%20Digital/Our%20Insights/Big%20data%20The%20next%20frontier%20for%20innovation/MGI_big_data_full_report.pdf.

55 IDB. 2018. *Cloud Computing: Opportunities and Challenges for Sustainable Economic Development in Latin America and the Caribbean.* https://publications.iadb.org/en/cloud-computing-opportunities-and-challenges-sustainable-economic-development-latin-america-and.

56 ITP.net. 2017. *UAE Appoints First Minister for Artificial Intelligence.* https://www.itp.net/615396-uae-appoints-first-minister-for-artificial-intelligence.

57 Digital Government Development Agency. https://www.dga.or.th/en/index.php.

Table 4: Improvement Opportunities Across the Seven Policy Enablers in the Focus Countries

Improvement opportunity by country: ▮ Large ▮ Medium ▮ Limited

Policy Enabler	Cambodia	Indonesia	Myanmar	Philippines	Thailand
Strategic governance	The government is in the process of developing a digital economy framework, which includes promoting data-driven governance	The Ministry of Research and Technology developed a national strategy for AI development to promote the use of big data in the public and private sectors	The Myanmar Digital Economy Roadmap has been completed; however, there is limited focus on big data	A cross-ministerial task force has been set up to draft the country's AI road map	The Digital Economy Promotion Agency (DEPA) is working with other government agencies to promote big data usage
Availability and quality of data	Score 17/100 with distance to frontier of 81% for open government data	Score 25/100 with distance to frontier of 72% for open government data	Score 1/100 with distance to frontier of 99% for open government data	Score 30/100 with distance to frontier of 67% for open government data	Score 34/100 with distance to frontier of 62% for open government data
Risk mechanisms	No comprehensive data protection law	Data protection law is under development	No comprehensive data protection law	Data Privacy Act was passed in 2012, but there have been concerns around enforcement	Personal Data Protection Act (PDPA) was developed in 2019, but enforcement has been postponed
Human capital for big data	Score 33/100 with distance to frontier of 67% for ICT skills[a]	Score 61/100 with distance to frontier of 39% for ICT skills[a]	Score 2.3/7 with distance to frontier of 56% for quality of STEM education[a]	Score 77/100 with distance to frontier of 23% for ICT skills[a]	Score 54/100 with distance to frontier of 46% for ICT skills[a]
Access to relevant technologies	Score 32/100 with distance to frontier of 68% for adoption of emerging technologies[a]	Score 59/100 with distance to frontier of 41% for adoption of emerging technologies[a]	Score 2.7/7 with distance to frontier of 59% for availability of latest technologies[a]	Score 52/100 with distance to frontier of 48% for adoption of emerging technologies[a]	Score 61/100 with distance to frontier of 39% for adoption of emerging technologies[a]
Data-driven culture	Score 31/100 with distance to frontier of 69% for government promotion of emerging technologies[a]	Score 61/100 with distance to frontier of 39% for government promotion of emerging technologies[a]	Score 2.9/7 with distance to frontier of 58% for importance of ICT to government vision[a]	Score 39/100 with distance to frontier of 61% for government promotion of emerging technologies[a]	Score 65/100 with distance to frontier of 35% for government promotion of emerging technologies[a]
ICT infrastructure	Score 44/100 with distance to frontier of 56% for investment in emerging technologies[a]	Score 63/100 with distance to frontier of 37% for investment in emerging technologies[a]	Score 2.8/7 with distance to frontier of 54% for ICT use by government to improve efficiency[a]	Score 61/100 with distance to frontier of 39% for investment in emerging technologies[a]	Score 54/100 with distance to frontier of 46% for investment in emerging technologies[a]

AI = artificial intelligence, ICT = information and communications technology, STEM = science, technology, engineering, and mathematics
[a] Distance to frontier refers to the percentage gap between the country's performance and the global best performing country on that indicator.
Sources: Global Open Data Index; Portulans Institute's Network Readiness Index 2020; World Economic Forum's Networked Readiness Index 2016; Literature review; AlphaBeta analysis.

enhance data management practices.[58] In Indonesia, there has also been a shift to online services in many government offices across the country over the past 5 years, with business licensing and civil registration services (e.g., providing national identity cards) leading the way.[59] Furthermore, the Ministry of Research and Technology has launched a national strategy to promote the use of big data in the public and private sectors, including health, education, and food security.[60] Meanwhile, in the Philippines, the E-Government Masterplan 2022 was launched by the Department of Information and Communications Technology (DICT) in 2019 to promote the digital transformation of government services, enhancing intergovernmental

---

[58] Digital Economy Promotion Agency (DEPA). https://www.depa.or.th/en/home.
[59] K. Walton and H. Rahemtulla. 2020. At Your Service: Indonesia's Government Agencies Look to Digital Innovations Amid COVID-19. *Asian Development Blog*. 5 November. https://blogs.adb.org/blog/your-service-indonesia-s-government-agencies-look-digital-innovations-amid-covid-19.
[60] D. Rahman. 2020. Indonesia Works On Use of Big Data for Better Decision-Making Process. *The Jakarta Post*. 15 October. https://www.thejakartapost.com/news/2020/10/15/indonesia-works-on-use-of-big-data-for-better-decision-making-process.html.

coordination, and improving the capacity of government agencies in utilizing ICTs in their operations.[61] The government also established a cross-ministerial task force composed of seven agencies to develop the country's AI road map, which is expected to be implemented in 2021.[62] The road map aims to transform the country into an "AI center for excellence," leveraging its local talent pool and entrepreneurship ecosystem.[63] In Cambodia, the government has developed a long-term digital transformation strategy.[64] Under the digital government pillar, the framework outlines the importance of data-driven governance, including leveraging big data applications.

- **Availability and quality of data.** There is a need to broaden access to data and improve the quality of data to capture the full potential of big data applications. This includes adopting open data policies, improving data collection processes, creating an integrated data platform to facilitate data sharing between government agencies, as well as improving collaboration mechanisms for private sector engagement. Based on the Global Open Data Index which assesses the availability and openness of government data across multiple aspects such as ease of access, cost of access, frequency of updates, and technical usability (e.g., machine-readable format), the five focus countries have varying levels of data availability. Thailand scored 34, the Philippines 30, followed by Indonesia at 25 out of 100.[65] Cambodia scored lower at 17 and Myanmar 1 out of 100. The five focus countries showed a gap of between 62% and 99% to the frontier or the best-performing country assessed. In some countries, while the government has been collecting multiple datasets, there is a lack of a system to standardize, consolidate, and share them to across different agencies. To date, several initiatives to improve data availability and quality have been observed across these countries. For example, in Thailand, the government announced a plan to collect and standardize data from 20 ministries into a centralized system to facilitate the use of data in policymaking and improve transparency.[66] Meanwhile, Cambodia Data Exchange (CamDX) is an important initiative by the Government of Cambodia to improve data collection and data sharing. CamDX curates data from different information systems into a unified and decentralized data exchange platform to provide a secure and standardized way of accessing data (Box 9).[67] Furthermore, mechanisms to engage the private sector are crucial to improving access to innovative datasets. This approach has been implemented in Indonesia and the Philippines. In Indonesia, Bappenas has partnered with the United Nations to launch Pulse Lab Jakarta, a joint facility to pilot innovative data solutions through partnering with the private sector and academia. Using datasets drawn from mobile communications, remote sensing, and social media, Pulse Lab Jakarta has generated insights for policymaking on topics ranging from fuel subsidies to natural disasters.[68] ADB and Gojek have signed a collaboration agreement to conduct joint research on the impact of digitization and COVID-19 on the operations and development of Indonesia's micro, small, and medium enterprises, leveraging Gojek's big data.[69] The Government of the Philippines also partnered with Grab to develop OpenTraffic, a smart data platform that provides free-of-cost GPS information for better analysis of travel speeds and journey times in Metro Manila and Cebu City. The real-time GPS data from Grab drivers could be used to address traffic congestion and identify road incident blackspots to improve emergency response timing.[70]

---

61 Government of the Philippines, Department of Information and Communications Technology. 2019. *E-government Masterplan 2022.* https://dict.gov.ph/ictstatistics/wp-content/uploads/2019/07/EGMP_Book_Abridged.pdf.

62 A. Parrocha. 2019. Gov't Crafting AI Road Map to Improve PH Productivity. *Philippine News Agency.* 17 July. https://www.pna.gov.ph/articles/1075265.

63 K. Crismundo. 2020. DTI Targets to Roll Out AI Roadmap Next Year. *Philippine News Agency.* 7 October. https://www.pna.gov.ph/articles/1117823.

64 T. Vireak, 2021. *Digital Policy Framework Launched.* 8 June. The Phnom Penh Post. https://www.phnompenhpost.com/business/digital-policy-framework-launched.

65 Global Open Data Index. https://index.okfn.org/.

66 K. Tortermvasana. 2018. Big Data Panel to Direct Country's Digital Transition. *Bangkok Post.* 1 March. https://www.bangkokpost.com/business/1420115/big-data-panel-to-direct-countrys-digital-transition.

67 CamDX. https://camdx.gov.kh/.

68 Global Pulse. *Pulse Lab Jakarta.* https://www.unglobalpulse.org/lab/jakarta/.

69 ADB. *ADB, Gojek to Initiate Research on Digitization, COVID-19 Impact on MSMEs.* https://www.adb.org/news/adb-gojek-initiate-research-digitization-covid-19-impact-msme.

70 *Grab.* 2016. Philippines: Real-Time Data Helps Philippine Government Improve Traffic Management in Major Cities. 5 April. https://www.grab.com/sg/press/social-impact-safety/philippines-real-time-data-helps-philippine-government-improve-traffic-management-in-major-cities/.

Box 9: CamDX—An Integrated and Secure Data Exchange Platform to Enable Big Data Usage

Designed based on the X-Road model of Estonia, CamDX connects fragmented information systems into an ecosystem to promote data exchanges in a standardized and secure way. The main goal of CamDX is to build an infrastructure that allows for easy access to data in government databases without compromising the security and ownership of the data.

As a data exchange platform, CamDX does not store or know the content of the data, but instead allows each member to connect with information systems of other members and exchange data directly through a secure server. The platform also establishes a foundation for collaboration between the public and private sectors. Government databases such as population and business registries as well as tax, real estate, and/or vehicle registration can be used in combination with data from telecommunication companies, banks, and insurance companies for purposes such as electronic Know Your Customer.

CamDX has so far supported two important applications in Cambodia—Online Business Registration (OBR) and Validation Application on Payment Guarantee:

- OBR is a new business registration platform that allows business owners to register and obtain the licenses to operate their business using a single portal. Through CamDX, the portal can efficiently distribute the data registered by business owners to respective information systems of Ministry of Commerce, Ministry of Interior, General Department of Taxation, and Ministry of Labour and Vocational Training, thereby reducing the cost and time of business registration. The first phase of the OBR has been completed, with an estimated approval time of 8 days and a 40% reduction in the registration fee.
- Validation Application on Payment Guarantee allows companies registered in Cambodia to provide a guarantee for their staff to enter Cambodia with "fast lane" during the COVID-19 pandemic, a special lane at airports that exempts travelers from a deposit and an insurance policy related to COVID-19 upon arrival to Cambodia.[a] The application forms submitted by companies are verified against data such as tax identification number, company name, and shareholder information from various government agencies through CamDX, including General Department of Taxation and Council for Development of Cambodia.

[a]   Government of Cambodia, Validation Application on Payment Guarantee (VAPG). 2020. *User Manual.* https://vapg. registrationservices.gov.kh/VAPG_USER_MANUAL.pdf.

- **Risk mechanisms.** Mechanisms need to be put in place to allow data sharing while minimizing the risk of unintended consequences such as data privacy infringements, security violations, and unethical usage of data. In the health and social welfare and protection sectors, for example, it is critical to impose strict data privacy and data security requirements to prevent breaches of sensitive information such as health records and social security data. On the other hand, governments also need to balance data protection with the need to facilitate data sharing during crises such as natural disasters or pandemics to support crisis management. To address these concerns, a comprehensive set of data protection laws needs to be developed and effectively enforced to address the risks associated with using big data while allowing for efficient sharing of data during crises that require timely and actional insights. Across the five focus countries, while data protection laws have been developed in several countries, there is a need to strengthen the enforcement of these laws to ensure personal data are protected. For example, while the Philippines' Data Privacy Act was passed in 2012, there have been concerns around the enforcement of the law and how data breaches and data privacy violations were resolved.[71] In Thailand, the Personal Data Protection Act was developed in 2019, however, the enforcement of most chapters of the law has

[71]   J. Santos. 2020. Philippine Privacy Regime Fails to Live Up to Expectations. *MLex.* 14 October. https://mlexmarketinsight.com/insights-center/editors-picks/area-of-expertise/data-privacy-and-security/philippine-privacy-regime-fails-to-live-up-to-expectations.

been postponed due to the COVID-19 pandemic.[72] Meanwhile, data protection laws in Indonesia and Cambodia are currently absent or still under development. For instance, the Personal Data Protection Bill in Indonesia, which aims to provide a comprehensive set of provisions for the protection of personal data both via electronic and nonelectronic systems, is being finalized by the Indonesian House of Representatives.[73] In Cambodia, while data protection is covered under different laws (e.g., Civil Code of Cambodia), there is a lack of comprehensive data protection legislation.[74]

- **Human capital for big data.** Building capacity of public sector employees is key to realizing the potential of big data. Governments need to implement initiatives in education and training to increase the pipeline of graduates with the right skills who can join the civil service. In particular, it is crucial to expand the supply of talents with advanced digital skills such as data science and machine learning to take advantage of big data applications. The five focus countries have varying levels of human capital readiness. Across three different indicators—UN E-Government Development Index,[75] Coursera's Global Skills Index,[76] and Portulans Institute's Network Readiness Index,[77] Indonesia, the Philippines, and Thailand scored relatively higher than Cambodia and Myanmar (Table 5). However, most countries still showed considerable gaps in terms of human capital as compared to the best-performing country in each index. This could be driven by the lack of trained talents in data-related fields as well as the lack of mechanisms to attract and retain these talents in the public sector. There have been several initiatives to address these gaps across the countries. For example, Thailand has introduced programs to develop big data capacity of public sector personnel. The DEPA is leveraging its newly created Government Big Data Institute to train government officers from different departments on big data skills.[78] Initiatives to equip government employees with big data skills in other countries are being planned or undertaken in small scale. For example, under the Philippine Statistical Development Program (PSDP) 2018–2023, which aims to strengthen the country's statistical capability through exploring the use of big data, there are plans to implement training programs for their staff on the use of open-source statistical software and statistical computing to take advantage of big data in monitoring the United Nations Sustainable Development Goals (SDGs).[79] In Cambodia, its digital transformation strategy places an important emphasis on developing a skilled workforce in specialized technology areas such as big data analytics, AI, and internet of things.

---

[72]   K. Tortermvasana. 2020. Most Parts of PDPA to be Deferred by a Year. *Bangkok Post*. 20 May. https://www.bangkokpost.com/business/1920972/most-parts-of-pdpa-to-be-deferred-by-a-year.

[73]   PwC. 2020. *Digital Trust NewsFlash*. https://www.pwc.com/id/en/publications/digital/digital-trust-newsflash-2020-02.pdf.

[74]   ZICO. 2019. *Personal Data Protection in ASEAN*. https://zico.group/wp-content/uploads/resources/asean_insiders/ASEAN_Insiders-PDPA.pdf.

[75]   The UN E-Government Development Index provides a comparative assessment of the e-government development of 193 UN Member States across different criteria, one of which is the human capital required for digital government development. United Nations. UN E-Government Development Knowledgebase. https://publicadministration.un.org/egovkb/en-us/Data-Center (accessed 10 December 2020).

[76]   The Global Skills Index developed by Coursera benchmarks skills proficiency of registered learners across 60 countries; one of the skills assessed is data science. Coursera. 2020. *Global Skills Index*. https://pages.coursera-for-business.org/rs/748-MIV-116/images/gsi2020_final.pdf.

[77]   The Network Readiness Index 2020 assesses the performance of 134 economies based on 60 indicators across Technology, People, Governance, and Impact, one of which is the level of ICT skills (e.g., computer skills, basic coding, digital reading). Portulans Institute. 2020. *The Network Readiness Index 2020*. https://networkreadinessindex.org/wp-content/uploads/2020/11/NRI-2020-V8_28-11-2020.pdf.

[78]   Government Big Data Institute (GBDI). https://gbdi.depa.or.th/.

[79]   Cai Ordinario. 2018. PHL Meets "Big Data" Challenges Through PSDP 2018–2023. *Business Mirror*. 1 November. https://businessmirror.com.ph/2018/11/01/phl-meets-big-data-challenges-through-psdp-2018-to-2023/.

Table 5: Levels of Human Capital Readiness in the Focus Countries

Country	UN E-Government Development Index – Human Capital Sub-index[a]		Coursera's Global Skills Index – Data Science Skills[a]	Portulans Institute's Network Readiness Index – ICT Skills	
	Score out of 1 (Max score = 1)	Rank out of 193	Rank out of 60	Score out of 100 (Max score = 100)	Rank out of 134
Cambodia	0.5	153	NA[a]	33	107
Indonesia	0.7	101	56	61	49
Myanmar	0.5	159	NA[a]	NA[a]	NA[a]
Philippines	0.8	83	31	77	21
Thailand	0.8	72	38	54	63

ICT = information and communications technology, UN = United Nations.
[a] Data are not available as the country was not assessed.
Sources: UN E-Government Development Index; Coursera's Global Skills Index; Portulans Institute's Network Readiness Index; AlphaBeta analysis.

- **Access to relevant technologies.** To enable big data adoption, it is necessary to ensure that government agencies are provided with access to relevant technologies to store, process, and analyze big data. According to the Portulans Institute's Network Readiness Index, which examined the level of adoption of emerging technologies such as big data analytics and cloud computing, the focus countries could see considerable improvement opportunities in terms of increasing access to technologies.[80] In particular, Cambodia, Indonesia, the Philippines, and Thailand were assessed to have a distance to the frontier[81] of between 39% and 68%.[82] Some countries are exploring the use of open-source software, software that is developed, tested, and improved through public collaboration, as a cost-effective approach to derive insights from big data. For instance, Cambodia is proposing the use of the Hadoop system which provides open-source tools for storing, processing, and analyzing big data in government agencies.[83] In the Philippines and Thailand,

---

[80] Assessment for Myanmar was conducted based on its score on availability of latest technologies in World Economic Forum's Networked Readiness Index 2016 due to data availability. See: World Economic Forum. 2016. *Networked Readiness Index.* http://reports.weforum.org/global-information-technology-report-2016/networked-readiness-index/?doing_wp_cron=1607413873.0174689292907714843750.
[81] This refers to the percentage gap between the country's performance and the global best performing country on that indicator.
[82] Portulans Institute. 2020. *The Network Readiness Index 2020.* https://networkreadinessindex.org/wp-content/uploads/2020/11/NRI-2020-V8_28-11-2020.pdf.
[83] S. Vor. 2020. *How Data-Driven Technology Can Upgrade Cambodia's E-government.* https://www.kas.de/en/web/kambodscha/single-title/-/content/how-data-driven-technology-can-upgrade-cambodia-s-e-government.

the study that estimated poverty levels using satellite data made use of PyTorch, a free and open-source software solution developed by Facebook, to analyze satellite imagery through deep-learning algorithms.[84]

- **Data-driven culture.** It is important for countries to instill a culture of making policy decisions on the basis of rigorous evidence. A paradigm shift at the highest level of government may be required to promote a data-driven culture and increase awareness of applications and technologies used in managing and analyzing data. There are currently considerable gaps in terms of promoting emerging technologies and applications (e.g., big data analytics, AI, machine learning, and cloud computing) across the focus countries (Table 4). To date, some countries have taken steps to foster a data-driven culture within government through developing a strategic road map for data-driven governance or even establishing an agency dedicated to promoting the use of data in policymaking. For example, the Philippines is promoting data-driven governance with its ICT Statistics Roadmap 2020–2022, a 3-year plan to create a robust evidence base to guide the country's ICT development policies and initiatives.[85] In Thailand, the DEPA has been tasked to raise awareness of big data applications and improve data management practices across government agencies.

- **ICT infrastructure to support big data.** The application of big data requires a strong ICT infrastructure that is capable of collecting, storing, transferring, and processing large amounts of data at extremely faster rates as compared to traditional data systems. It is, therefore, necessary to invest in ICT infrastructure, in particular, improving cloud computing capabilities in government to provide a cost-effective and scalable way to store big data and enable efficient cloud-based big data analytics. The current level of investment in ICT infrastructure varies across countries, however, there exist sizable gaps that need to be addressed, particularly in Cambodia and Myanmar (Table 4) (footnote 80). The countries are taking actions to improve the quality of ICT infrastructure to support digital transformation, including big data applications. For instance, the Ministry of Public Health in Thailand is leveraging cloud infrastructure to store health data from various sources, which can be efficiently accessed to support big data applications.[86] With its Cloud First policy, the Philippines is also encouraging all government agencies to move to cloud computing as the preferred ICT deployment strategy for internal administrative use and external delivery of government services.[87] Meanwhile, under the digital transformation strategy of Cambodia, the government has also placed an emphasis on developing ICT infrastructure to build a foundation for digital transformation.

▶ **Targeted policy reforms could strengthen country performance on the key policy enablers.**

Based on the assessment of key policy enablers in the previous section and a review of government initiatives in each of the five focus countries, a number of policy reforms have been identified. Table 6 shows a summary of the specific policy reform recommendations and their relevance for each country.

---

84 Y. Sawada and E. Tan. 2020. Meeting Development Challenges with Trusted Data. *Asian Development Blog*. 20 October. https://blogs.adb.org/blog/meeting-development-challenges-trusted-data.

85 Government of the Philippines, Department of Information and Communications Technology (DICT). 2020. *Data-Driven ICT Governance*. https://dict.gov.ph/ictstatistics/wp-content/uploads/2020/10/Data-Driven-ICT-Governance-NICTHS-2019_final.pdf.

86 Government of Thailand, Ministry of Public Health. *Thailand Healthcare Digital Transforming*. https://www.ispor.org/docs/default-source/conference-ap-2018/thai-1st-plenary-for-handouts.pdf?sfvrsn=268f61e4_0.

87 Government of the Philippines. GOV.PH. *Department Circular: Cloud First Policy*. https://www.gov.ph/web/integrated-government-philippines-program/policies/signed/department-circular-cloud-first-policy; and Department of Information and Communications Technology (DICT). https://dict.gov.ph/dict-releases-amended-cloud-first-policy-for-govt-transition-to-new-normal/#:~:text=The%20Philippine%20Government's%20Cloud%20First,and%20cost%2Defficiency%20among%20users .

Table 6: Relevance of Recommendations for the Focus Countries

Degree of relevance:[a]   ■ High   ■ Medium   ■ Low

Policy Enabler	Policy Recommendation	Cambodia	Indonesia	Myanmar	Philippines	Thailand
Strategic governance	1. Designate a digital transformation champion in government	Medium	Medium	High	Medium	Low
	2. Establish a national multi-stakeholder task force	High	High	High	High	High
Availability and quality of data	3. Create integrated data platforms (i.e., one stop-shops) for open big data	High	High	High	High	High
	4. Establish forums to interact and crowd-source data from the private sector	High	Low	High	High	High
Risk mechanisms	5. Establish data protection frameworks	High	Medium	Medium	Medium	High
	6. Collaborate with international community on common standards and approaches	High	High	High	High	High
Human capital	7. Provide targeted training and incentives for civil servants to acquire relevant skills	High	High	High	High	High
Access to relevant technologies	8. Establish mechanisms to crowd-source innovations and technologies	High	High	High	High	High
Data driven culture	9. Provide incentive schemes for data-driven decision-making	High	High	High	High	Medium
Information and communications technology infrastructure	10. Go 100% cloud first for government	High	High	High	Low	Medium

[a] The degree of relevance was assessed by combining the scores in Table 4 with a review of government initiatives across the five focus countries. Where governments were found to have well-established programs related to the recommendation, relevance was set to "Low"; where there were early plans, but no implementation had begun or the plans had been implemented in small scale, the assessment was set to "Medium"; Relevance was high if the assessment of policy enablers showed a significant improvement opportunity and the country had no active plans of similar policies.

Sources: Review of existing government initiatives; AlphaBeta analysis.

The following is an explanation of the policy levers that have been assessed as most relevant to achieving each opportunity and potential policy recommendations:

1. **Policy reforms for improving strategic governance.** Improving strategic governance will involve two aspects: installing clear senior leadership on who is overseeing the implementation of big data applications in public services delivery as well as involving a multisector group of stakeholders in the process.
   - **Designate a digital transformation champion in government.** Countries should identify a clear lead official or lead agency that drives the digital transformation process and the adoption of big data in government. The analogy would be a Chief Data Officer or Chief Information Officer in

private sector organizations. The appointment of a senior official to this position ensures that various government services are linked to each other and that information between government ministries are shared. The champion also plays a role in standardizing operating procedures across government departments. A key risk to avoid is to appoint champions that may have public visibility, but lack decision-making powers making the role essentially superficial. One way of ensuring this does not occur is to provide support from the highest levels of government (e.g., Prime Minister or President's office), as has been the case in the digital transformation of Singapore, as well as establishing clear reporting lines and granting the appointed digital champions the necessary powers. Countries are already making progress on this. In Thailand, the DGA and the DEPA have stepped into this role and Cambodia, with the support of ADB, has convened a transitional "Big Data Sub-Committee" which is chaired by the Secretary of State of the Ministry of Economy and Finance. Similarly, Indonesia's Ministry of Research and Technology which is leading the national strategy to promote big data usage and the Philippines's DICT which launched the E-Government Masterplan 2022 is taking lead in promoting digital transformation in these countries.

- **Establish a national multistakeholder task force.** It is important to set up a multistakeholder task force involving different government agencies as well as the private sector and academia to foster collaboration and explore big data applications that can be used to improve public service delivery. Not only will such multistakeholder promote innovative approaches due to a broad set of inputs, but it will also ensure that national big data ambitions tie into sector-specific road maps and address coordination challenges across sectors. Once a multistakeholder task force is established to lead the big data transformation process on the policy front, the next step is to appoint a department or agency to be in charge of the implementation of big data strategies and road maps on the ground. In addition, it is also critical to have strong engagement with the private sector such as industry associations, technology companies, and start-ups, as well as ensure that there is a strong fact based on the specific challenges and local context that will shape the implementation in each sector.[88] While some of the focus countries have taken steps in convening a platform involving different government agencies as well as the private sector (e.g., Thailand's Digital Economy Promotion Agency is working with other government agencies to promote big data and Big Data Sub-Committee in Cambodia is participated by both public and private sector representatives), there is currently a lack of multistakeholder task force with clearly defined roles and strategies to engage various partners in driving big data adoption in the country. These initial efforts should be expanded in each country to establish a multistakeholder task force which brings together government agencies, private sector, and academia to explore and test big data applications in priority sectors.

2. **Policy reforms for improving availability and quality of data.** Countries are required to improve the availability and quality of data to enable meaningful big data applications. This could involve creating an integrated platform for open big data to facilitate cross-ministerial and cross-sector data sharing, as well as improving mechanisms to partner with and crowd-source data from the private sector. To ensure that open data efforts result in impactful and practical applications, it is important that governments engage the private sector and citizens to identify the most relevant data that need to be collected and analyzed to avoid investing in data that are not useful for stakeholders, which have been noted as a concern in the past across Southeast Asia.[89]

---

[88] McKinsey Global Institute. 2010. *How to Compete and Grow: A Sector Guide to Policy.* https://www.mckinsey.com/~/media/McKinsey/Industries/Public%20and%20Social%20Sector/Our%20Insights/How%20to%20compete%20and%20grow/MGI_How_to_compete_and_grow%20A_sector_guide_to_policy_Exec_Summary.pdf; and Eden Strategy Institute. *Five Considerations When Planning Your Sector Development Roadmap.* https://www.edenstrategyinstitute.com/2018/12/31/five-considerations-when-planning-your-sector-development-roadmap/.

[89] ASEAN Secretariat. 2016. *Masterplan on ASEAN Connectivity 2025.* https://asean.org/storage/2016/09/Master-Plan-on-ASEAN-Connectivity-20251.pdf.

- **Create integrated data platforms (i.e., one-stop shops) for open big data.** Having a single portal to access information can play a crucial role in disseminating data. Singapore, for example, operates an Open Data Resources portal that provides access to an array of government data from over 70 public agencies, direct developer support, and special subportals for data from tax authorities, land transport, monetary authority, and geo-spatial data, to name a few.[90] Colombia also operates an open data resources portal ("Datos Abiertos Colombia") that provides access to an array of government data from over 1,200 public agencies, developer support, and special subportals for niche data from government entities.[91] Furthermore, the interoperability of data should be improved to create synergies from existing databases collected by various government agencies. For example, in the Philippines, data from the Philippine Identification System, the government's central identification platform, can be combined with data from social protection programs and health data to establish a unified beneficiary database.[92] In addition, countries could consider creating a distributed model where data are stored in different information systems and can be shared via a data exchange layer. Box 10 shows an example of such a model which has been implemented in a number of countries.

Box 10: X-Road—A Data Exchange Layer that Enables Unified and Secure Data Sharing

X-Road is a centrally managed distributed Data Exchange Layer between information systems, which allows organizations to exchange information over the internet while ensuring confidentiality, integrity, and interoperability between data exchange parties. Originally developed and launched by the Estonian State Information Systems Department (at the Ministry of Economy and Communications) in 2001, the model has so far been expanded and implemented in a number of countries in Europe, Africa, Asia, and Latin America.[a]

X-Road was developed to address the issue of information silos where data are generated and administered separately by different government agencies. The platform allows authorized agencies to exchange important data in an efficient and secure manner while maintaining the integrity and confidentiality of data while it is in transit.[b] X-Road is resilient to cyberattacks and service interruptions as data are stored locally by data exchange parties and no third parties have access to the data.[c] X-Road's distributed architecture also makes it highly scalable and is, therefore, a good fit for all sizes of implementation. A number of trainings and e-resources are made available online for the public to learn about the X-Road data exchange layer. X-Road also provides X-Road Playground, which allows any individual or organization to test a preconfigured X-Road environment free of charge.

The X-Road model was adopted by Cambodia to develop CamDX, a unified and decentralized data exchange layer that has supported several government digital services. CamDX was built and set up locally in the data center of the Ministry of Economy and Finance. The implementation of CamDX has also involved other ministries such as the Ministry of Commerce, General Department of Taxation, and Ministry of Labour and Vocational Training which provide data on businesses, the Ministry of Interior which allows CamDX to verify Khmer National Identification, as well as the Council for the Development of Cambodia which allows CamDX to combine investment data with company registration data.[d]

[a] X-Road. https://x-road.global/xroad-history.
[b] E-Estonia. https://e-estonia.com/solutions/interoperability-services/x-road/.
[c] Nordic Institute for Interoperability Solutions (NIIS). https://www.niis.org/blog.
[d] CamDX. https://camdx.gov.kh/#what_is_camdx.

[90] Smart Nation Singapore. *Open Data Resources.* https://www.smartnation.sg/resources/open-data-resources.
[91] Datos Abiertos Colombia. https://www.datos.gov.co/en/.
[92] Philippine Statistics Authority. https://psa.gov.ph/philsys/faqs.

- **Establish forums to interact and crowd-source data from the private sector.** Governments should engage and empower private sector organizations to participate in sharing data. While it can be challenging to establish data sharing agreements between the government and the private sector, pilot programs could be created to test potential public–private partnerships before engaging in long-term agreements. One potential approach is to establish a "data insights unit" that can work across different government agencies and with the private sector as well as academic partners to mobilize data and test potential applications of big data. A similar model has been implemented in Indonesia and can be expanded across the focus countries to foster collaboration and mobilize resources (Box 11).

Box 11: Crowd-Sourcing Data through a "Data Insights Unit"

A "data insights and innovations unit" could be established to connect different government agencies with the private sector as well as academic partners to mobilize resources and cocreate practical big data solutions. This will help demonstrate potential applications of big data and allow the government to incorporate them in their existing operations. A similar model has been implemented in Indonesia, and resulted in a number of collaborations and pilot programs to test the application of big data in public service delivery.

Founded in 2012, Pulse Lab Jakarta is a joint data innovation facility bringing the Government of Indonesia its development partners (e.g., the United Nations and World Bank) as well as the private sector (e.g., Grab, Visa, and Twitter) and academia together to explore and promote the adoption of data-driven applications. Leveraging various data sources such as mobile communications, remote sensing, and social media, Pulse Lab Jakarta has generated insights for policy and practice on a range of topics related to development and humanitarian actions (e.g., disaster response and climate change, food security and agriculture, and financial inclusion). This model has successfully mobilized data insights from the private sector to support policymaking. For example, Pulse Lab Jakarta partnered with Grab to analyze drivers' anonymized global positioning system traces in Greater Jakarta to create a set of interactive visualizations of traffic flows across different subdistricts. Leveraging the partnership with Grab, further research was conducted to show the feasibility of using ride-hailing data to inform transportation policy and planning, as well as to develop proxy measures of air quality.

Source: Pulse Lab Jakarta. https://pulselabjakarta.org/ourwork.

3. **Policy reforms for improving risk mechanisms.** Mechanisms are needed to minimize the risk of unintended consequences such as data privacy infringements, IP concerns, and unethical usage of data. However, decisions regarding data privacy and protection vary by country context, perceived values, and potential for misuse. It is important to ensure that policy addresses public concerns while not relying on overly restrictive regulations.
   - **Establish data protection frameworks.** Comprehensive data protection frameworks need to be developed and effectively enforced to address the risks associated with using big data. For example, the United States introduced the Health Information Technology for Economic and Clinical Health Act to encourage health care providers to adopt health information technology while improving the protection of electronic health records through increased penalties for violation of privacy and security rules.[93] In Canada, the Privacy Act ensures that the government collects, uses, and discloses personal information according to strict rules that preserve individuals' right to privacy.[94] It is also important to balance data protection with the

---

[93]   Government of the United States, Department of Health and Human Services. *HITECH Act Enforcement Interim Final Rule.* https://www.hhs. gov/hipaa/for-professionals/special-topics/hitech-act-enforcement-interim-final-rule/index.html.

[94]   Office of the Privacy Commissioner of Canada. *The Privacy Act.* https://www.priv.gc.ca/en/privacy-topics/privacy-laws-in-canada/the-privacy-act/pa_brief/.

need to ensure efficient sharing of critical data during times of crises (e.g., sharing personal location data during pandemics to support disease tracking). In the Republic of Korea, for example, this was achieved through a set of supportive legislation that allows the sharing of personal data during a public health crisis. In particular, the Infectious Disease Control and Prevention Act allows authorities to access personal data that could help prevent the spread of infectious diseases, including credit card transactions and travel, medical, and location records from public and private organizations.[95] Countries also need to ensure strong data governance in public-private collaboration. In the Pulse Lab Jakarta model, for example, data protection is incorporated into innovation projects through Risks, Harms, and Benefits Assessments which are designed to identify anticipated or actual ethical and human rights issues that may occur at any stage of a data innovation process. The tool also helps develop a risk mitigation strategy and ensure that the risks do not outweigh the benefits of a given project.[96] When it comes to the implementation of data protection measures, there are opportunities to leverage new technologies such as blockchain to manage access to and use of public sector data while maintaining the security of this information. Estonia provides a relevant case in point with its Keyless Signature Infrastructure. Keyless Signature Infrastructure leverages blockchain technology to safeguard public sector data including electronic health records of all Estonian citizens by allowing government officials to track and monitor changes within various databases (e.g., who changed a record, what changes were implemented, and when they were made).[97] IT departments in government agencies may also be able to create rules and algorithms that allow data in a blockchain to be automatically shared with third parties once predefined conditions are met.

- **Cooperate with the international community on common standards and approaches.** Standards are particularly crucial to not only ensure some minimum safeguards for safety and security around data. In the United States, for example, memoranda are used to update security protocols for data released by federal agencies, providing adequate controls to ensure that information is "resistant to tampering, to preserve accuracy, to maintain confidentiality as necessary, and to ensure that the information or service is available as intended by the Agency and as expected by users."[98] Standards are also particularly crucial for easing international cooperation, given that data may be utilized across borders. Standards impact everything from security issues to the provision of open data. For example, adopting international security and privacy standards not only assists governments in the design and development of their own frameworks, but also provides comfort and reassurance to organizations. Furthermore, having common standards decreases the barriers for domestic firms to export their operations abroad, as their security standards are likely to already comply with international markets, and vice-versa reduces the barriers to entry for foreign firms for the same reasons. Cooperating on standard setting can also facilitate the provision of open data. For example, the ASEAN Secretariat is currently developing an open data dictionary (with common standards across the ASEAN Member States) to share available government data with the public (footnote 89). Even if international standards are adopted, however, it is important that countries engage in thorough reviews with extensive local and international stakeholder consultations (with industry and standards governing bodies in particular) to solicit feedback and ensure that standards are fit for the local context.

4. **Policy reforms for improving human capital.** Building capacity of public sector employees is key to realizing the potential of big data. Governments need to put in place education initiatives to increase the pipeline of graduates with the right skills who can join the civil service. In addition, it is crucial to

95   C. Chang. 2020. How South Korea Used Tech to Track Down Coronavirus and Curb Spread. *The Straits Times.* 1 May. https://www.straitstimes.com/asia/east-asia/how-south-korea-used-tech-to-track-down-virus-and-curb-spread.

96   Pulse Lab Jakarta. https://pulselabjakarta.org/ourwork.

97   S. Cheng et al. 2017. Using Blockchain to Improve Data Management in the Public Sector. *McKinsey Digital.* 28 February. https://www.mckinsey.com/business-functions/mckinsey-digital/our-insights/using-blockchain-to-improve-data-management-in-the-public-sector#:~:text=Over%20time%2C%20blockchain%20can%20help,a%20blockchain%20to%20be%20automatically.

98   IDB. 2016. *Big Data in the Public Sector: Selected Applications and Lessons Learned.* https://publications.iadb.org/publications/english/document/Big-Data-in-the-Public-Sector-Selected-Applications-and-Lessons-Learned.pdf.

provide training for existing civil servants to equip them with the necessary skills required to make data-driven decisions. Governments should also leverage big data expertise of the private sector.

- **Provide targeted training and incentives for civil servants to acquire relevant skills.** There is a significant lack of data science skills in the five focus countries in general, not to mention the public sector. Countries need to develop strategies to increase the availability of such skills, particularly among public sector employees to enable them to make data-driven decisions. This could involve providing training for civil servants on data management and analysis skills. For example, the United Kingdom launched a Data Science Accelerator program in 2015 which offers training in a range of data analysis techniques for people working in government, with a particular focus on the National Health Service.[99] Across the focus countries, there have been initiatives to train government officials on relevant skills in Thailand and the Philippines which could be expanded and replicated in other countries (the DEPA and Government Big Data Institute in Thailand provided training on big data skills while the DICT in the Philippines conducted the National Training of Trainers on data-driven governance for participants from both central and local governments).[100] To ensure the effectiveness of training programs, countries will need to identify credible courses that offer well-structured training on relevant skills from introductory to advanced levels (e.g., online resources could be leveraged to lower costs and allow for better access and flexibility). For instance, in the United States, the Federal Data Science Training Program run by the Office of Management and Budget has launched a program to teach government employees data science skills such as coding, graph analytics, and data visualization and ethics, which will be conducted entirely online.[101] The Philippines has also emphasized the use of e-learning platforms in building the digital capacity of government in its 2021 Budget Priorities Framework.[102] It is recommended to focus initial efforts on providing targeted training for officials who work in dedicated data-related agencies (e.g., government data offices and data insights units), and subsequently expand the coverage of such training (e.g., through "train-the-trainer" model). Countries could leverage private sector expertise in conducting training for government officials. For example, the Government Technology Agency of Singapore has been partnering with Tableau since 2017 to train and deepen public officers' capabilities in data analytics and visualization.[103] In addition, to encourage civil servants to engage in upskilling activities, governments could consider incentives such as providing flexible time-off to attend training, establishing mechanisms to recognize training efforts as key milestones for career progression (e.g., offering promotion and salary increases for people who obtain certifications in data skills), and offering scholarships to those who want to deepen their knowledge and skills through further studies. In the Public Service Division in Singapore, for example, employees can attend up to 100 hours of training, of which 60% should be related to their current job responsibilities while the remaining 40% can be for personal development or to prepare themselves for their future career in the service.[104] Scholarships are also made available under the Training Awards and Sponsorships Scheme for postgraduate, degree, and diploma courses. However, a major risk associated with such programs is the loss of talents to the private sector after they have obtained important data skills. This could be addressed by requiring people who receive training and scholarships to take up a commitment to work in the public sector for a certain period after they finish their programs.

---

[99] Data Science Campus. *Data Science For Public Good–Data Science Accelerator.* https://datasciencecampus.ons.gov.uk/capability/data-science-accelerator/.

[100] UNESCAP. *Philippines Training Of Trainers On Data-Driven Governance.* https://www.unescap.org/events/philippines-training-trainers-data-driven-governance.#.

[101] D. Nyczepir. 2020. Federal Data Science Training Program will Make Use of Coronavirus Datasets, Be Entirely Online. *Fedscoop.* 4 August. https://www.fedscoop.com/data-scientist-training-omb-coronavirus/.

[102] Government of the Philippines, Department of Budget and Management. 2021. *2021 Budget Priorities Framework.* https://www.dbm.gov.ph/images/Briefer-on-2021-Budget-Priorities-Framework-05262020.pdf.

[103] Tableau. *GovTech and Tableau Renew Partnership to Deepen Data Skills in Singapore's Public Service.* https://www.tableau.com/about/press-releases/2020/govtech-and-tableau-renew-partnership-deepen-data-skills-singapores-public.

[104] Government of Singapore, Public Service Division. *Learning and Development Opportunities.* https://www.psd.gov.sg/join-us/career-growth-and-development/learning-and-development-opportunities.

5. **Policy reforms for improving access to relevant technologies.** Working with big data requires adequate technologies and analytical techniques, i.e., software. Many of which exist in the private sector or in research, but are often proprietary and not accessible to governments. Many current data analysis tools are neither suitable nor effective at dealing with large datasets. This could be addressed by establishing mechanisms to crowd-source innovations and technologies from the private sector, academia, and even citizens.

   - **Establish mechanisms to crowd-source innovations and technologies.** While multistakeholder task forces and forums will be important to provide access to innovations and technologies currently not present in government, the five focus countries will need to go beyond this. Possible approaches include providing incentives for public sector innovations, encouraging open-source research, improving transparency around government procurement of technologies, and providing regulatory flexibility for experimentation and pilots. For example, while not targeted at big data specifically, Bangladesh's "Innovation for All (a2i)" fund provides financing for low-cost, user-centric, homegrown innovations to leverage digital innovation to solve policy problems. To date, a total of $4.5 million worth of grants have been awarded to government agencies, development organizations, nongovernmental organizations, academic institutions, private companies, and even individuals to design and implement their solutions across 22 development areas such as agriculture, environment, education, health, and government services.[105] This has resulted in a number of innovations being implemented on the ground (e.g., solar-powered multimedia classrooms have been set up in off-grid locations, an online platform for Environment Clearance Certificate has been implemented to facilitate the application process, and a 3D printer has been used to print artificial limbs for disabled children from low-income families). Furthermore, there is a need to improve the transparency of how governments will reward the private sector or eventually procure big data solutions developed by the private sector (i.e., what is the monetization model for developing AI solutions and machine learning algorithms for the public sector). Before big data solutions are launched at a large scale, they first need to be piloted and evaluated within a defined environment. This may require the use of regulatory sandboxes which allow time-bound testing of big data approaches in the real world. Box 12 provides a more detailed explanation of how regulatory sandboxes can be used to promote innovations.

Box 12: Establishing Regulatory Sandboxes to Promote Innovations

A regulatory sandbox provides an environment for companies to test innovative products, services, or business models within a clearly defined space (e.g., for a limited period with a limited number of users). Following successful testing, companies can make their new products, services, or business models available to a wider customer base. These sandboxes are useful policy tools to understand the implications of introducing certain new analytical tools and applications while continuing to promote technological innovation and limiting any negative unforeseen consequences (i.e., breaches of data privacy or potential harmful biases of artificial intelligence applications). They can help regulators better understand new approaches and work collaboratively with the private sector to develop appropriate rules and regulations for emerging big data solutions. From a private sector perspective, sandboxes reduce the costs of production and time-to-market. When structuring the sandboxes, it is important to have early engagement with the private sector, research and academic institutions, civil society, and consumer protection agencies to evaluate their potential impact. Furthermore, a thorough review process is required to assess the costs and benefits of innovations before bringing lessons from pilot sandboxes into broad-based implementation.

Source: Financial Conduct Authority. Regulatory Sandboxes. https://www.fca.org.uk/firms/innovation/regulatory-sandbox.

---

[105] access to information (a2i). *Innovation Lab is Changing the Scenario.* https://a2i.gov.bd/innovation-lab/.

6. **Policy reforms for improving data-driven culture.** Countries need to develop a culture that promotes and rewards evidence-based policymaking, which refers to establishing policies grounded on objective and scientific research and ensuring they are designed and implemented based on concrete data.[106]

   • **Provide incentive schemes for data-driven decision-making.** For government agencies and individual civil servants to change to a more data-driven culture requires incentives for such change, i.e., policy makers need to have "skin in the game." There are several approaches that can be considered, one of which is around tying promotions and career progress to using data in decision-making. South Africa, for example, introduced performance rewards linked to the use of data in decision-making in government.[107] Competition amongst different government entities could be another method. Different agencies can be empowered to develop their own big data solutions to address common challenges (e.g., poverty reduction) based on real-world context.[108]

7. **Policy reforms for improving information and communications technology (ICT) infrastructure to support big data.** Working with big data requires adequate technological infrastructure. Governments that intend to use big data will thus need improved ICT infrastructure to store, organize, and process complex data sets in an efficient manner.

   • **Go 100% cloud first for government.** Cloud has emerged as an ideal computing environment for big data as it provides vast quantities of computing power at low cost and on a need basis, without major hardware investments. Furthermore, an increasing number of software tools held in a hybrid cloud are also capable of performing the processing and data integration tasks.[109] Cloud computing can also lead to significant efficiency gains and cost savings for governments' ICT budgets beyond the importance of big data. For example, Saudi Arabia's Ministry of Communications and Information Technology has put forward a "Cloud First Policy" which encourages government entities to consider cloud solutions first for every new IT investment—this is expected to provide around 30% cost savings of the total cost of ownership.[110] Across the focus countries, the Philippines has launched a Cloud First policy to encourage all government agencies to move to cloud computing for internal administrative use and external delivery of government services—such initiative could be developed in other countries to develop the necessary infrastructure for big data.

▶ **Five pilot programs for using big data in health care, social welfare and protection, and education can be prioritized for the focus countries.**

Based on an assessment of various big data opportunities across health care, social welfare and protection, and education, five opportunities have been identified for potential pilot programs in the five focus countries. Box 13 describes the methodology used to select the five big data pilot programs.

---

[106] Kim et al. 2019. Big Data Analytics in Government: Improving Decision Making for R&D Investment in Korean SMEs. *Sustainability.* 12 (1). https://www.mdpi.com/2071-1050/12/1/202.

[107] AlphaBeta and the Bill & Melinda Gates Foundation. 2018. *Digital Innovation in Public Financial Management (PFM): Opportunities and Implications for Low-Income Countries.* https://www.alphabeta.com/wp-content/uploads/2018/07/pfm-technology-paper-summary-version.pdf.

[108] D. Esty and R. Rushing. 2007. The Promise of Data-Driven Policymaking. *Issues in Science and Technology.* XXIII (4). https://issues.org/esty-2/.

[109] ADB. 2019. Readiness of National Statistical Systems in Asia and the Pacific for Leveraging Big Data to Monitor the SDGs. *ADB Briefs* No. 106. March. https://www.adb.org/sites/default/files/publication/491326/adb-brief-106-national-statistical-systems-big-data-sdgs.pdf.

[110] Government of Saudi Arabia, Ministry of Communications and Information Technology. 2019. *KSA Cloud First Policy.* https://www.mcit.gov.sa/sites/default/files/ksa_cloud_first_policy_en.pdf.

Box 13: Methodology Used to Select Big Data Pilot Programs

The big data applications identified in the previous section were assessed against three criteria to select the most suitable applications for pilot programs:

1. **Evidence of impact.** This was assessed through literature research and interviews with relevant stakeholders to identify examples of each opportunity (including research studies and pilot programs). The level of evidence is determined based on whether there are examples of such application in relevant countries (i.e., low or middle-income countries).
2. **Access to data.** This was assessed based on whether the data required in each big data opportunity is already available across the five focus countries (e.g., social media data and satellite data) or it needs to be collected by the government (e.g., digital health records) or obtained through collaboration with the private sector (e.g., traffic data from shared mobility platforms).
3. **Relevance.** The relevance of each big data opportunity was assessed based on a combination of qualitative (e.g., literature review of progress and existing gaps in each country) and quantitative methods (e.g., assessment of indicators such as the number of active coronavirus disease (COVID-19) cases in the population and the mortality rate of noncommunicable diseases). This was supplemented by a review of existing government initiatives to understand if the application is relevant to the local context and is aligned with government priorities (e.g., rolling out vaccines).

Source: Authors.

Table 7 shows a summary of the assessment results for the five opportunities that have been prioritized for the focus countries. See Table A4 of Appendix 4 for detailed methodology.

Below is an explanation of each prioritized opportunity for potential pilot programs in the five focus countries.

- **Using social media and search data to analyze COVID-19 activity.** Leveraging real-time data from social media and search engines to analyze COVID-19 activity is highly relevant for the five focus countries, particularly in Indonesia, Myanmar, and the Philippines where the number of active cases in population is significantly higher than the Southeast Asia average.[111] In particular, as of mid-December 2020, Indonesia had over 94,000 active cases, the highest in the region, while the Philippines had more than 24,000 and Myanmar had more than 18,000 active cases.[112] The application of social media data to track infectious disease activity has proven feasible in a number of countries. For example, the study conducted in Greece described in the previous section showed the potential of using both Twitter data and Google data to track influenza activity and predict the emergence of possible outbreaks.[113] In addition, there have been several studies in the People's Republic of China to explore the use of real-time data such as Baidu searches to analyze COVID-19 activity, predict potential infections, and locate high-risk areas. In a study that analyzed Baidu searches related to COVID-19 (e.g., using key words such as dry cough, fever, chest distress, coronavirus, and pneumonia) from December 2019 to February 2020, it was found that search data could predict new suspected COVID-19 cases 6 to 9 days earlier.[114] To enable such application, countries need to obtain a large amount of social media data, which can be accessed through Application Programming Interfaces (APIs) of social media companies. In the study of influenza activity in Greece, for instance, Twitter data were obtained using Twitter STREAMING API while search data were collected from Google

---

[111] Worldometer. https://www.worldometers.info/coronavirus/#countries (accessed 16 December 2020).
[112] WHO. WHO Coronavirus Disease (COVID-19) Dashboard. https://covid19.who.int/ (accessed 10 December 2020).
[113] L. Samaras et al. 2020. Comparing Social Media and Google to Detect and Predict Severe Epidemics. *Scientific Reports*. 10 (1). pp. 1–11. https://www.researchgate.net/publication/339959031_Comparing_Social_media_and_Google_to_detect_and_predict_severe_epidemics.
[114] L. Qin et al. 2020. Prediction of Number of Cases of 2019 Novel Coronavirus (COVID-19) Using Social Media Search Index. *International Journal of Environmental Research and Public Health*. 17 (7). p. 2365. https://www.researchgate.net/publication/340321213_Prediction_of_Number_of_Cases_of_2019_Novel_Coronavirus_COVID-19_Using_Social_Media_Search_Index.

Trends, a tool that provides access to an anonymized sample of Google search data. There is a potential opportunity to conduct a pilot study to explore the use of social media data in analyzing COVID-19 activity in the most affected countries such as Indonesia and the Philippines. The Philippines, for example, has also highlighted the use of big data analytics to understand the spread of diseases (e.g., COVID-19) to streamline medical care and allow for real-time collection and analysis of health data in the updated Philippine Development Plan 2017–2022.[115]

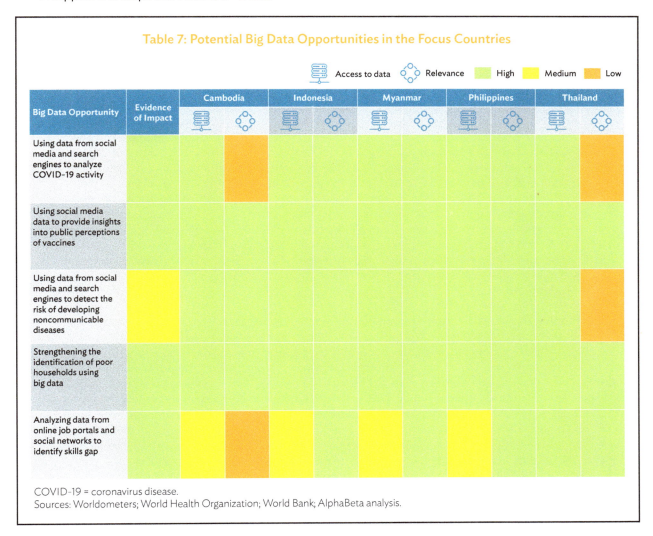

Table 7: Potential Big Data Opportunities in the Focus Countries

COVID-19 = coronavirus disease.
Sources: Worldometers; World Health Organization; World Bank; AlphaBeta analysis.

- **Using social media data to provide insights into public perceptions of vaccines.** To curb the spread of COVID-19, all five countries have announced plans to purchase and roll out vaccines to the broader population. For example, the Philippines aims to commence vaccinations from June 2021 and expects to inoculate about 25 million people (about 25% of its population) over the course of the year.[116] Thailand has

115 Government of the Philippines. GOV.PH. *Philippine Development Plan.* http://pdp.neda.gov.ph/wp-content/uploads/2021/02/Pre-publication-copy-Updated-PDP-2017-2022.pdf.
116 Dezan Shira & Associates. 2020. COVID-19 Vaccine Roll Outs in ASEAN & Asia–Live Updates by Country. *ASEAN Briefing.* 16 December. https://www.aseanbriefing.com/news/covid-19-vaccine-roll-outs-in-asean-asia-live-updates-by-country/.

been conducting COVID vaccinations since February 2021[117] while Cambodia has signed up for COVID-19 Vaccines Global Access and has procured vaccines through private purchases to support its goal of completing vaccine rollout by June 2022 or before.[118] Understanding public perceptions of vaccines is particularly crucial to enable effective vaccine rollout. This could be achieved by analyzing real-time social media data such as Twitter conversations, which can be obtained through the company's API. Such analysis proved to yield valuable insights as shown in a study conducted by the Government of Indonesia and its development partners (e.g., information about public concerns around vaccination such as religious issues and side effects of vaccines, identification of influencers that could be leveraged for rapid response to public concerns, and misinformation related to vaccines) (see the previous section). This analysis could be applied across the five focus countries to provide insights into public perceptions around COVID-19 vaccines.

- **Using data from social media and search engines to detect the risk of developing noncommunicable diseases.** While addressing noncommunicable diseases is a longer term goal for the five focus countries, it is an important public health issue that requires timely interventions. In particular, mortality rates from noncommunicable diseases across Cambodia, Indonesia, Myanmar, and the Philippines are considerably higher than the Southeast Asia average.[119] Big data can contribute to the prevention and detection of noncommunicable diseases by allowing public health authorities to monitor relevant risk factors and provide targeted interventions. For example, social media can provide timely community-level data on health information seeking and changes in behaviors, and can be combined with other data such as demographics, environment, diet, and physical activity indicators from other digital sources (e.g., mobile applications and wearables) to monitor health behaviors to supplement delayed estimates from traditional surveillance systems.[120] Social media data such as Twitter posts and search data from Google are valuable data sources that could be used for such analysis. A pilot study leveraging Twitter data and Google search data could be developed to explore the potential application of these datasets in monitoring noncommunicable diseases in the focus countries.

- **Strengthening the identification of poor households using big data.** Building a database of granular and updated poverty statistics is not only relevant to the focus countries in light of the current COVID-19 pandemic, but also critical in the long term to ensure effective targeting of vulnerable populations. This is particularly important where the shares of the population living below national poverty lines are relatively high at 13.5% for Cambodia, 25% for Myanmar, and 16.7% for the Philippines.[121] The study conducted by ADB in the Philippines and Thailand has shown the potential of using innovative datasets such as satellite imagery to complement traditional statistics in identifying poor households. This could be expanded to other countries through a pilot program to test the effectiveness of satellite data in mapping different poverty profiles. The program could rely on publicly accessible satellite imagery and open-source data analytics tools to demonstrate the feasibility of the approach to national statistics offices and policy makers.

---

[117] National News Bureau of Thailand. 2021. *Thailand Raises Vaccine Supply Target to 150m Doses.* https://thainews.prd.go.th/en/news/detail/TCATG210508164907683.

[118] Dezan Shira & Associates. 2020. COVID-19 Vaccine Roll Outs in ASEAN & Asia–Live Updates by Country. *ASEAN Briefing.* 16 December. https://www.aseanbriefing.com/news/covid-19-vaccine-roll-outs-in-asean-asia-live-updates-by-country/; and WHO. *172 Countries and Multiple Candidate Vaccines Engaged in COVID-19 Vaccine Global Access Facility.* https://www.who.int/news/item/24-08-2020-172-countries-and-multiple-candidate-vaccines-engaged-in-covid-19-vaccine-global-access-facility.

[119] WHO. *Total NCD Mortality.* https://apps.who.int/gho/data/view.main.2490 (accessed 18 December 2020).

[120] N. Cesare et al. 2019. Use of Social Media, Search Queries, and Demographic Data to Assess Obesity Prevalence in the United States. *Palgrave Communications.* 5 (1). pp. 1–9.

[121] World Bank. *Poverty Headcount Ratio at National Poverty Lines (% of Population).* https://data.worldbank.org/indicator/SI.POV.NAHC (accessed 18 December 2020). It is based on official government sources or World Bank calculations. For Cambodia, the information is sourced from World Bank country overview. https://www.worldbank.org/en/country/cambodia/overview.

- **Analyzing data from online job portals and social networks to identify skills gap.** The use of data from job portals and social networks such as LinkedIn to identify skills gap and develop training programs to equip students and workers with in-demand skills is highly relevant to the focus countries, both during the COVID-19 pandemic as well as when economies start to recover. To address unemployment issues caused by COVID-19, Thailand has started analyzing data from job portals to build a database of skill needs, which will be used to develop programs to re-train the workforce (see the previous section). A similar approach could be implemented in other countries to identify in-demand skills and guide education and training efforts. This will potentially involve partnerships with online job portals to obtain data on jobs and skills. In addition, there is also a potential opportunity to partner with social network sites such as LinkedIn to provide insights into the labor market situation in each country. Such collaboration was piloted in South Africa, which resulted in important insights that enabled the government to identify emerging skills and develop strategies to produce a pipeline of talent in these areas.

SECTION IV

Conclusion

Digital transformation would be critical for governments to undertake economic recovery in the post-pandemic environment. Big data could be a key tool to help countries initiate their digital transformation. This report provides policy recommendations on how big data can be used by public institutions in three public service sectors—health care, social welfare and protection, and education. These recommendations could help the focus countries in their post-COVID economic recovery and contribute to the existing plans of ADB, such as its Strategy 2030.

Digital technologies are an important element in ADB's Strategy 2030.[122] For example, "promoting innovative technology" is one of ADB's guiding principles. Moreover, digital technologies can play an important role in helping ADB address its operational priorities. For example, one of its seven operational priority is "addressing remaining poverty and reducing inequality" through "improving education and training." As discussed in the report, big data can play a key role in improving education. For instance, by leveraging big data analytics, schools can look into the vast number of student records to identify early warning signs and provide targeted support to those in need.

To distinguish between "low-hanging fruits" that governments can capture in the near term versus policies that require longer timeframes to implement and take effect, the policy recommendations in the report have been further analyzed in terms of their implementation timeframe. This takes into account multiple factors including the policy's potential for short-term impact and political feasibility.

The policy recommendations have been prioritized as follows:
- **Short-term.** Implementation should begin within the next 12 months as these actions are important for providing the foundation for other actions, and have the potential for near-term impact. The first step is to establish strategic governance mechanisms such as designating a digital transformation champion in government and establishing a national multistakeholder task force to drive big data adoption. For example, lessons from other countries and consultations with policy advisors and big data experts highlighted the risks of pilot programs not being effective if governance mechanisms are not present to ensure they are prioritized appropriately and there are follow-up actions to scale-up the implementation.
- **Medium-term.** Implementation should begin over the next 1–2 years as these actions rely to some extent on the short-term actions. These include creating integrated data platforms and forums to crowd-source data from the private sector, developing data protection frameworks and collaborating with the international community on common standards and approaches, and providing targeted training and incentives for civil servants to acquire relevant skills. As countries are at different stages of readiness, the specific implementation timelines of these policy actions will also depend on the capacity and priorities of each government.
- **Long-term.** Implementation can take place over the next 3–5 years as these actions require more resources and long-term commitment from government. These include developing cloud first policies, providing incentive schemes for data-driven decision-making in government (e.g., performance rewards linked to the use of data in decision-making), and establishing mechanisms to crowd-source innovations and technologies (e.g., improving public procurement guidelines and establishing regulatory sandboxes). While such actions are expected to result in significant long-term impact, they require strong political will and a whole-of-government approach to be effective.

---

[122] ADB. 2018. *Strategy 2030: Achieving a Prosperous, Inclusive, Resilient, and Sustainable Asia and the Pacific.* Manila. https://www.adb.org/sites/default/files/institutional-document/435391/strategy-2030-main-document.pdf.

Appendixes

APPENDIX 1

Assessment of the Potential Value of Big Data

The potential value of big data was for each sector based on four criteria:
- **Volume of data.** The larger the amount of data in the sector, the more it indicates the potential to benefit from utilizing big data analytics. This depends not only on the volume of potential data, but how much is currently digitized.
- **Variety of data.** The more different forms of data available in the sector (e.g., social media, video content, and structured data), the more potential value there could be in combining them to generate unique insights.
- **Veracity of data.** The higher the quality or accuracy of the data, the better the potential insights.
- **Value of applications.** The degree to which there are specific applications in that sector that can deliver value.

Table A1 provides a discussion of the methodology used to assess the potential value of big data in each sector based on these criteria.

Table A1: Methodology Used to Assess the Potential Value of Big Data by Sector

Criteria	Assessment		
	High	Medium	Low
Volume of data	Large potential amount of data generated in the sector with high degree of digitization	Large potential amount of data generated in the sector, but low degree of digitization	Limited amount of data generated in the sector
Variety of data	Large potential variety of data in different forms and there are examples or theoretical concepts in the literature of combining them to generate insights	There are some forms of data that can be combined to generate insights	Limited variety of data that can be combined to generate insights
Veracity of data	All forms of data generated in the sector have high quality and accuracy	The quality and accuracy of data vary (i.e., some forms of data are accurate and reliable while others are not)	Data generated in the sector generally has low quality and accuracy
Value of applications	There are various use cases of big data to support decision-making in the sector, including real examples of such applications	There are some use cases of big data to support decision-making in the sector and most are theoretical concepts	There are limited use cases of big data to support decision-making in the sector

Source: Authors.

APPENDIX 2

Sizing of Opportunities from Using Data-Driven Technologies

The potential opportunities brought about by data-driven technologies were sized for the health and education sectors across 10 Southeast Asian countries. Tables A2.1 and A2.2 summarize the key metrics and sources used to size of the potential benefits of data-driven technologies in the health and education sectors by 2030.

Table A2.1: Metrics and Sources Used for Opportunity Sizing in the Health Sector

Applications	Metrics and Methodology	Sources
1. Application of remote patient monitoring systems to improve patient care	Sized based on cost savings to the health care system through reduced hospital visits, length of patients' stays, and medical procedures. McKinsey Global Institute (MGI) suggests 10% to 20% savings to the health care system from the resultant reduced hospital visits, length of patients' stays, and the number of procedures relating to chronic diseases. Country-level estimates are based on total health care spend based on World Bank data and the share of spending on chronic diseases.	MGI[a] World Bank[b]
2. Use of data analytics tools to direct highly targeted public health interventions for at-risk populations	Sized based on the economic value of reduced disability-adjusted life years due to timely public health interventions. MGI indicates that the most significant and measurable impacts are on maternal and child health, as well as public sanitation and hygiene. It estimates a 0.4% reduction in disability-adjusted life years for "high-income" countries, and 1.6% for other countries. Countries are classified by income based on the World Bank's definition. Economic value is taken to be this multiplied by GDP per capita, and is estimated based on the proportion of the population suffering from chronic diseases. Country-level estimates are based on national population sizes and GDP per capita.	MGI[a] UN Population Division[c] World Bank[d]

GDP = gross domestic product, UN = United Nations.
[a] McKinsey Global Institute. 2013. *Disruptive Technologies: Advances that Will Transform Life, Business, and the Global Economy.* https://www.mckinsey.com/business-functions/digital-mckinsey/our-insights/disruptive-technologies.
[b] World Bank. https://data.worldbank.org/indicator/SH.XPD.CHEX.GD.ZS.
[c] UN Population Division. https://esa.un.org/unpd/wpp/DataQuery/ (accessed 10 December 2020).
[d] World Bank. https://blogs.worldbank.org/opendata/new-country-classifications (accessed 10 December 2020).

Table A2.2: Metrics and Sources Used for Opportunity Sizing in the Education Sector

Applications	Metrics and Methodology	Sources
1. Online platforms where job openings are posted, and compatible candidate profiles are matched to available jobs based on algorithms	Sized based on GDP contributions from increased employment rates. MGI estimates the impact on employment rates of different countries, stating that these are different for each country, depending on its labor market characteristics, education and income levels, and demographic trends. Country-level estimates are based on national employment rate, labor force, and GDP per capita.	MGI[a]
2. Use of digital technologies to provide personalized and remote learning opportunities for students	Sized based on increased GDP from increased employment. MGI estimates that these levers would lead to an increase in employment rate by 0.5% in high-income countries and 0.9% in other countries. Classification of "high income" countries is based on the World Bank's definition. Country-level estimates are based on national employment rate, labor force, and GDP per capita.	MGI[a] World Bank[b]

GDP = gross domestic product, MGI = McKinsey Global Institute.
[a] McKinsey Global Institute. 2015. *A Labor Market that Works: Connecting Talent with Opportunity in the Digital Age.* https://www.mckinsey.com/featured-insights/employment-and-growth/connecting-talent-with-opportunity-in-the-digital-age.
[b] World Bank. https://blogs.worldbank.org/opendata/new-country-classifications (accessed 10 December 2020).

APPENDIX 3

Assessment of Policy Enablers for Big Data

The improvement opportunities with regard to the seven policy enablers for big data were assessed for each of the focus countries based on a review of existing government policies and strategies as well as a range of international indices. Table A3 provides a summary of the methodology used for the assessment of each policy enabler.

Table A3: Methodology Used for Assessment of Policy Enablers

| Policy Enablers | Metrics/Sources | Improvement Potential | | |
		Large	Medium	Limited
Strategic governance	Review of existing government strategies and road maps related to big data	No road map or designated agency related to big data applications in government	Road map is in process of being developed or at the early stage of implementation; lack of a lead agency to promote big data in government	Presence of clear road map and designated agency to drive big data applications in government
Availability and quality of data	Assessment of country scores in terms of availability and openness of government data across multiple aspects such as ease of access, cost of access, frequency of updates, and technical usability (Global Open Data Index)	Distance to frontier of more than 50%	Distance to frontier of between 20% and 50%	Distance to frontier of less than 20%
Risk mechanisms	Review of existing data protection and data privacy laws	No data protection or privacy laws in place	Some data protection/privacy laws established, but incomplete or significant gaps	Robust data protection and privacy laws established providing clear guidance on use of data
Human capital for big data	Assessment of country scores in terms of ICT skills (Portulans Institute's Network Readiness Index 2020[a])	Distance to frontier of more than 50%	Distance to frontier of between 20% and 50%	Distance to frontier of less than 20%
Access to relevant technologies	Assessment of country scores in terms of adoption of emerging technologies (Portulans Institute's Network Readiness Index 2020[b])	Distance to frontier of more than 50%	Distance to frontier of between 20% and 50%	Distance to frontier of less than 20%

continued on next page

Table A3: *continued*

Policy Enablers	Metrics/Sources	Improvement Potential		
		Large	Medium	Limited
Data-driven culture	Assessment of country scores in terms of government promotion of emerging technologies (Portulans Institute's Network Readiness Index 2020[c])	Distance to frontier of more than 50%	Distance to frontier of between 20% and 50%	Distance to frontier of less than 20%
ICT infrastructure	Assessment of country scores in terms of investment in emerging technologies (Portulans Institute's Network Readiness Index 2020[d])	Distance to frontier of more than 50%	Distance to frontier of between 20% and 50%	Distance to frontier of less than 20%

ICT = information and communications technology.

[a] Assessment for Myanmar was conducted based on its score on quality of science, technology, engineering, and mathematics education dimension in World Economic Forum's Networked Readiness Index 2016 due to data availability.

[b] Assessment for Myanmar was conducted based on its score on availability of latest technologies in World Economic Forum's Networked Readiness Index 2016 due to data availability.

[c] Assessment for Myanmar was conducted based on its score on importance of ICT to government vision in World Economic Forum's Networked Readiness Index 2016 due to data availability.

[d] Assessment for Myanmar was conducted based on its score on ICT use by government to improve efficiency in World Economic Forum's Networked Readiness Index 2016 due to data availability.

APPENDIX 4
Prioritization of Big Data Applications

A list of potential big data applications was assessed against a set of criteria to select the most suitable applications for pilot programs (Table A4).

Table A4: Big Data Applications Assessed

Big Data Applications		Data Required	Countries with Evidence[a]
Health care	Using data from social media and search engines to analyze influenza activity	Social media and search data which can be accessed publicly or purchased	Greece, People's Republic of China, and Republic of Korea
	Using data from smartphone-connected thermometers to track influenza activity and detect emergence of possible epidemics	Data from smartphone-connected thermometers which can be obtained through collaboration	United States
	Using location and transport data as well as credit card transactions for contact tracing	Data from telecom service providers, transport providers, financial institutions, and citizens	People's Republic of China and Republic of Korea
	Using social media data to provide insights into public perceptions of vaccines	Social media data which can be accessed publicly or purchased	Indonesia
	Using data from hospitals and population studies to detect the risk of developing noncommunicable diseases	Multiple databases and health records from hospitals, public health agencies, and population studies	European Union
	Using data from social media and search engines to detect the risk of developing noncommunicable diseases	Social media and search data which can be accessed publicly or purchased	United States
	Using data from remote monitoring systems to improve productivity and reduce patient in-hospital bed days	Data from sensors to monitor heart conditions, blood-sugar levels, temperatures	People's Republic of China; Singapore; and Taipei,China
Social welfare and protection	Strengthening the identification of poor individuals and households using big data	Satellite data and/or data from mobile phone operators (e.g., mobility, use of services and applications, monthly expenditure)	Mexico, the Philippines, and Thailand
	Improving program design by analyzing historical data of social welfare programs to identify gaps and develop more tailored approaches	Electronic records of background of beneficiaries, interventions conducted, benefits received, and impact of past programs	Germany
Education	Analyzing data from online job portals and social networks to identify skills gap and develop training programs	Job portal data which can be accessed publicly	Thailand
	Analyzing student records to identify signs of dropping out and provide targeted support to those in need	Electronic records of students' background, financial status, class attendance, and academic results	United States
	Analyzing data on students' learning styles, areas of interest, abilities, and progress to customize teaching methods and curriculums to individuals' needs	Data on students' interactions with virtual learning environments and academic records	United States

[a] This includes big data applications that have been implemented as well as exploratory research and/or pilot studies that have been conducted in the country.
Sources: Literature review; AlphaBeta analysis.

Three criteria were used to prioritize the most suitable big data applications:

1. **Evidence of impact.** This was assessed through literature research and interviews with relevant stakeholders to identify examples of each opportunity (including research studies and pilot programs). The level of evidence is determined based on whether there are examples of such application in relevant countries (i.e., low or middle-income countries).
2. **Access to data.** This was assessed based on whether the data required in each big data opportunity is already available across the five focus countries (e.g., social media data and satellite data) or it needs to be

collected by the government (e.g., digital health records) or obtained through collaboration with the private sector (e.g., traffic data from shared mobility platforms).

3. **Relevance.** The relevance of each big data opportunity was assessed based on a range of indicators such as the number of active coronavirus disease cases in the population and the mortality rate of noncommunicable diseases. For each indicator, the team evaluated whether there is a large gap between each of the focus countries and the Southeast Asia average. This is supplemented by literature research and a review of existing government initiatives to understand if the application is relevant to the local context and is aligned with government priorities (e.g., rolling out vaccines).

Table A5 provides an explanation of the methodology used in the assessment.

Table A5: Methodology for Prioritizing Big Data Applications

Criteria	Score		
	High	Medium	Low
Evidence of impact	There are examples (including research studies and pilot programs) of the big data application in relevant countries (i.e., low or middle-income countries)	There are examples of the big data application in developed countries or theoretical concepts of the application have been mentioned in the literature, but no specific examples of such application were found	There are no examples or theoretical concepts of the big data application mentioned in the literature
Access to data	Data required for the big data application is already available, and can be accessed publicly or purchased (e.g., satellite imagery, Twitter data, and Google search data)	Data required for the big data application needs to be obtained through partnering with the private sector (e.g., telecommunication companies and shared mobility companies) or collected by the government	It is unclear whether there are any mechanisms or infrastructure to collect the data required for the big data application in the assessed country (e.g., digital health records and data on students' interactions with e-learning platforms)
Relevance	There is a significant challenge in the assessed country (as compared to the Southeast Asia average) that can be addressed by the big data application (e.g., high number COVID-19 active cases and high poverty rate). In some cases, there is already a plan by the government to leverage big data in that area	The current state of the assessed country is similar to the Southeast Asia average (within 15% of the Southeast Asia average)	The current state of the assessed country is significantly better than the Southeast Asia average

COVID-19 = coronavirus disease.
Source: Authors.